Battleground Europe

UTAH BEACH

St Mère Église

Cover painting by James Dietz, AGAINST ALL ODDS, Ridgway's Troopers seize La Fière Causeway, 9 June, 1944.

Battleground Europe

UTAH BEACH
St Mère Église

Carl Shilleto

LEO COOPER

For Irena
This book is dedicated to the memory of
Sgt Joseph Z. Pritchett Jr., 531st ESR. KIA, 25 June, 1944
and to all the brave men of VII Corps
who lost their lives in the Normany Campaign

'Not in vain may be the pride of those who survived
and the epitaph of those who fell.' Winston Churchill, 1874-1965

Published by
LEO COOPER
an imprint of
Pen & Sword Books Limited
47 Church Street, Barnsley, South Yorkshire S70 2AS
Copyright © Carl Shilleto 2001

ISBN 0 85052 736 8

A CIP record of this book is available
from the British Library

Printed by Redwood Books Limited
Trowbridge, Wiltshire

For up-to-date information on other titles produced under the Leo Cooper
imprint, please telephone or write to:
Pen & Sword Books Ltd, FREEPOST SF5, 47 Church Street
Barnsley, South Yorkshire S70 2BR
Telephone 01226 734222

CONTENTS

ACKNOWLEDGEMENTS

To begin with I must first acknowledge and give most sincere thanks to the many veterans that have contacted me and with whom I have met in the course of my research. This thanks is not just for what they did, over half a century ago, during the dark years of the Second World War, but also for having the patience and time in responding to my numerous appeals and the many questions asked while I was collating information for this book. I must also offer my apologies to those whose interesting anecdotes I have not been able to use as a result of the inevitable editorial restrictions. To have met those Normandy veterans, and in some cases to have accompanied them around the battlefields, has been, and always will be, a great pleasure and a privilege.

I would also like to thank many others, who work behind the scenes in museum, record office and library archives, for their time and work is sometimes overlooked and often goes unrewarded. Their work, in preserving and cataloguing papers, documents and publications, is invaluable and is greatly appreciated by many historians.

While it would be impossible to mention everyone who has contributed to the completion of this book, by offering help, advice, information and the loan of valuable documents, photographs or publications, a few I would like to mention are: in France, Mr Joseph Rivers and Mr Michael W. Green, Normandy American Cemetery; Monsieur Philippe Jutras and Monsieur Foché, Musée de Troupes Aéroportées; Monsieur Charles de Vallavieille and Mme Séverine Letourneur, Musée du Débarquement d'Utah Beach; Monsieur Philippe Chapron, Musée Mémorial de la Battaille de Normandie; Staff at the Tourisme Information in St Mère Église and also Monsieur Franck Néthivien, Monsieur Jean Michel Selles and my friends William Moutafis, Corinne Lecourt and Pascaline Dagorn.

In the USA I wish also to thank: Brigadier-General Alvin D. Ungerleider, Mr Louis A. Pritchett, Mr Sam P. Daugherty, Mr Dan Fisher, Mr Harper C. Coleman, Mr Hobart Morris, Mr E. Carver McGriff, Mr Wallace E. Treadaway, Mr Roger L. Chagnon, Mr Arthur L. Herzberg, Mr Howard G. Devoe, Mr Stephen J. Semago, Mr Bob Babcock and Mr Milton D. Crippin. Also thanks to the staff and other members of the 4th Infantry Division and 82nd and 101st Airborne Division Associations.

In Great Britain I would like to thank Mr Charles Hewitt, Brigadier Henry Wilson and Roni Wilkinson, Pen & Sword Books Ltd; Mr Frank

S. Kaufmann, Cambridge American Cemetery; Mr Tony Rider, Normandy Veterans Association, South Devon and Torbay Branch; Mr Peter Southcombe, Carole Johnson, Mr Tim Almy, Helen Hartly, Angus Newbould, Stephen Mead and Ken Wintle. Thanks also to my friend and mentor Charles Whiting, for his tireless encouragement and for sharing his extensive knowledge on the Second World War, and his wife Irma for their hospitality.

Finally, special thanks to my two daughters, Michaela and Hannah, for putting up with a father who probably spends too many hours away from them while researching and writing. My special thanks also to Irena Zientek, MA MSc, for her help in reading through my manuscript, selecting photographs, and her constant encouragement.

To everyone I hope my work justifies all our efforts.

INTRODUCTION

Normandy today has such a high number of war memorials and plaques dedicated to the Allied forces that one can be forgiven for thinking that there is little need for any more.

However, during the course of my research in Normandy I became aware of a new organization that is dedicated to preserving the memory of not just one individual unit or division, but of every American serviceman who crossed the beaches of Utah or Omaha and fought for the liberation of north-west Europe.

In an area adjacent to the Utah Beach Museum, it is hoped that sufficient funds can be raised to build a memorial park which will have, when fully completed, sixteen circular memorial gardens. In each of the gardens there will be granite columns which together, will have engraved upon them the names of some 414,700 American servicemen.

The first phase will begin with the inscription of the 66,000 names of US veterans who had previously contributed $40 each to a organization known as the Battle of Normandy Foundation. This organization was meant to build a memorial wall, however, this project was never completed.

In its place the US World War Two Wall of Liberty Foundation was founded in 1997 to make this dream become a reality. To begin with twenty-three acres of land have already been donated by a French businessman, Monsieur Paul Louis Halley, with the promise of more land if needed.

The President of the Foundation, Brigadier-General Alvin D. Ungerleider, is himself a veteran who landed on Omaha Beach as a platoon leader with the 115th Infantry Regiment, 29th Infantry Division, on the 6th June, 1944. Later, he completed his distinguished service career by serving in both the Korean and Vietnam wars.

The Wall of Liberty has been designed by Monsieur Jean Baltrusaitis and has already been approved by United States Fine Arts Commission. The American Battle Monuments Commission has also given its approval for the Foundation to begin fund-raising.

When completed the Memorial Park will complement the Normandy American Cemetery and Memorial at Omaha Beach; where over 9,300 American Servicemen are buried, and veterans, families and visitors are provided with a peaceful and fitting surrounding where they can reflect upon the sacrifices, and accomplishments, of a past generation.

The Foundation is presently seeking donations to help achieve their aim of building the Wall of Liberty. Each granite section, which will contain 240 names, is being offered to benefactors at a price of $15,000 which will include recognition, at the site, for the individual or organization. For American contributors tax-free status has been granted by the IRS and, therefore, all donations are tax deductible.

However, any donation, no matter how small, will be gratefully accepted, and acknowledged, by the Foundation. These should be made payable to the 'US World War II Wall of Liberty Foundation' and posted to the following address: 'World War II Wall of Liberty Foundation', Foundation Headquarters, 5254 Signal Hill Drive, Burke, VA 22015-2164. USA.

Whatever contribution you can make, it is a small price to pay when compared to that which has been paid by the tens of' thousands of Allied soldiers, sailors and airmen that will remain, forever, buried in the battlefields of north-west Europe.

Carl Shilleto
St Mère Église, France.

ADVICE FOR VISITORS

Your visit to the area of operations for the US VII Corps will cover ground in the La Manche département of Normandy. This département covers some 2,295 square miles and has over 180 miles of coast line, however, this book concentrates on the north-eastern part of La Manche, on the Cotentin Peninsular, where the American Forces landed on D-Day the 6th June, 1944.

This part of Normandy has remained relatively underdeveloped since the Second World War and most of the land is used, as it has been for centuries, for farming and growing crops. Many of the concrete defences built by the Germans, as part of Hitler's *Festung Europa* (fortress Europe), are still in evidence today. Though most of the armaments have long since been removed and nature has overgrown most of the fortification sites, they nevertheless, in places, still manage to create a formidable presence. What they must have appeared like for the Allied soldiers who faced them when they were protected by barbed wire, minefields, machine-gun posts and anti-tank weapons we can, for most of us, only dare to imagine.

These remains of the Atlantic Wall, and the surrounding terrain, therefore, provide the visitor with a means of better understanding the battlefield and, more importantly, the difficulties faced by the American forces when they landed in this area in the early hours of the 6 June, 1944.

Travel

The best way to travel to this part of France is by using one of the ferry companies; either Brittany Ferries sailing from Portsmouth to Caen (6 hrs) and Poole to Cherbourg (4hrs 15 mins). Tel: 0990 360360, or P&O European Ferries sailing from Portsmouth to Cherbourg (5 hrs day & 7 hrs 15 mins night). Tel: 0990 980555.

For drivers, comprehensive insurance is advisable and you must also carry the registration documents (plus a letter of authority from the owner if it is not your vehicle). A full valid driving licence, current insurance certificate and international distinguishing sign are also required; plus, your headlights should be adjusted for right-hand driving.

There are a couple of rules that need to be observed while driving in France, the first being the priority rule. While most major roundabouts and junctions are the same as the UK, with priority given to the left, many towns still have priority from the right. These, however, will be marked with a yellow diamond signpost or the words 'Passage Protégé,' indicating that you have right of way. The second rule is that if someone flashes their headlights at you in France it generally means that they have priority, and not you; this is contrary to the standard practice in the UK.

Though the new autoroute, the N13, provides quick and easy travel to the major towns such as Cherbourg, Carentan and St Mère Église. Most of the roads used in this tour are not main roads and therefore extra care is needed while driving; particularly on the single-track lanes.

A cost effective way of travelling to Normandy can be to use one of the many coach travel companies that offer battlefield tours. Though your freedom of travel is limited, these tours, conducted by experienced guides, can provide an invaluable insight into the Normandy landings and allow you to observe the battlefield while someone else does the driving. Leger Holidays, Sunway House Canklow Meadows, Rotherham S60 2XR. Tel: 01709 839839 offer many such tours conducted by authors who write for the *Battleground Europe* Series.

Accommodation

There are many hotels to choose from in this region. Two, which are ideally located, are: Hôtel Le Sainte Mère at St Mère Église, which has forty-two rooms and a restaurant, Tel: 02.33.21.00.30. and the Hôtel Restaurant L'Estaminet, 50480 St-Marie-du-Mont, which has five rooms, Tel: 02.33.71.57.01.

Alternatively, an up-to-date brochure of hotels, camping sites and other accommodation can be obtained from the French Travel Centre, 178 Piccadilly, London WIV OAL. Tel: 0891 244123.
Website: www.franceguide.com.

The local Tourist Information Offices in France, called Office de Tourisme, Syndicat d'Initiative or Tourisme Information, can be located at Rue de Général de Gaulle, 50480 St Mère Église. Tel: 02.33.21.00.33; Boulevard de Verdun, 50500 Carentan. Tel: 02.33.42.74.01; and at Maison du Tourisme de Cherbourg et du Hait Cotentin, 2 Quai Alexandre III. Tel: 02.33.93.52.02.

Telephones

When telephoning France from the UK, dial 0033 and drop the first 0 on the local number. To call from the US or Canada, dial 011 33 and then drop the 0 on the local number. Emergency numbers in France are: 17 for the Police, 15 for an Ambulance and 18 for the Fire Brigade. The operator is 13 and Directory Enquiries is 12.

Useful Equipment

I recommend visiting the area covered in this book during the summer months when the weather is more agreeable, places of interest are open longer hours, and you are also seeing the environment in climatic conditions similar to those experienced by the troops during the Normandy invasion. The weather in Normandy is very similar to the British climate with unpredictable rainstorms and changes in temperature. Therefore, waterproofs, sturdy shoes or walking boots are essential and suncream advisable. Other useful additions to your travelling pack would be sunglasses, a small first-aid kit, a bottle of water, pen-knife, binoculars, camera, notebook and pencil (ink smudges in the rain), maps and a comfortable back-pack to carry it all in.

The most detailed maps of the area covered in this book, are the IGN SÉRIE BLUE (Series Blue) and you will need two to cover the area in Chapter Six; the 1311 O, 1:25000, St Mere Eglise map and the 1311 E, 1:25000 St-Marie-du-Mont (Utah Beach) map. Another useful map is the IGN 06, TOP 100, 1:100000 Caen, Cherbourg map, which covers all the landing beaches as well. These maps can all be ordered from WATERSTONES, 28/29 High Ousegate, York, YO1 1NP. Tel: 01904 628740.

Finally, while travelling around this area please be courteous to the local people and give due respect when looking around near their property or land; just as you would expect from any visitor to your country. If you are in any doubt whether an area of land is public or private property, then please ask the locals for advice. If you do not speak French then a good phrase book or dictionary is essential and a good piece of advice is to at least try and communicate in French. The effort, even if appalling, is appreciated and you will find the local people more helpful and hospitable as a result.

How Best to Use This Book

It would be advisable to read this book before you travel. This will help you become familiar with the operations of VII Corps and give you an idea of what there is to see in the area so that you can better plan your trip.

Normandy has a larger concentration of war memorials than any other battlefield in the world, and the reader will notice that the area covered in Chapters Four and Five, is also partially covered in Chapter Six. This, however, has been done intentionally so that the reader is not distracted from the story by the directions and information relating to the many memorials or plaques.

In fact, there are so many memorials in this area that it has been necessary to compile a separate appendix in order to list all those that are related to VII Corps. In addition, a glossary has also been compiled to help the reader recognise the many abbreviations used by the Allied and German forces and which, today, are used (but not explained) in many books and articles on the subject. Though by no means a comprehensive glossary, it does, however, cover all those terms which are used on the memorials and plaques in this area and on the information given in local museums.

To better understand the events experienced by the Allied and German forces, both in the build-up to and during the invasion, the words of veterans have been used throughout the text. It is my hope that by reading these first-hand accounts of the horrors and cost of war, that future generations will gain a better appreciation, and understanding, of the sacrifices that have been made for the freedom and liberty that is now so readily taken for granted.

GLOSSARY

1/501st Regiment	1st Battalion, 501st Parachute Infantry
2/8th	2nd Battalion 8th Infantry Regiment
AAA/AT	Anti-Aircraft Artillery/Anti-Tank
A/B	Airborne
AEB	Airborne Engineer Battalion
AMC	Airborne Medical Company
AOK	*Armee-Oberkommando* (Army HQ Staff)
Armd	Armoured
Asst	Assistant
AW	Automatic Weapons
BAR	Browning Automatic Rifle
Bn	Battalion
BODP	Beach Obstacle Demolition Party
Brig	Brigadier
Comdr	Commander
Co & Coy	Company
Col	Colonel
COS (CofS)	Chief of Staff

Cpl	Corporal
Div	Division
DZ	Drop Zone
E-boat	German Motor Torpedo Boat
ECB	Engineer Combat Battalion
Eng	Engineer
ESB	Engineer Special Brigade
ESR	Engineer Shore Regiment
FAB	Field Artillery Battalion
Feldwebel	German rank of Sergeant
FLAK	*Flugabwehrkanone* (anti-aircraft gun)
FSG	Fire Support Group
Gefreiter	German rank of Lance-Corporal
Gen	General
General	German rank of Lieutenant-General
Generalfeldmarschall	German rank of Field Marshal (UK) & General of the Army (US)
Generalleutnant	German rank of Major-General
Generalmajor	German rank of Brigadier-General
Generaloberst	German rank of General
GIAB	Glider Infantry Artillery Battalion
GIR	Glider Infantry Regiment
Hauptmann	German rank of Captain
HHB	Headquarters and Headquarters Battery
HQ	Headquarters
Inf	Infantry
JA	Joint Assault
JCS	Joint Chiefs of Staff
KIA	Killed in Action
lbs	Pounds in weight
LCA	Landing Craft Assault
LCC	Landing Craft Control
LCF	Landing Craft Flak
LCG	Landing Craft Gun
LCI	Landing Craft Infantry
LCM	Landing Craft Mechanized
LCS	Landing Craft Support
LCT	Landing Craft Tank
LCT (R)	Landing Craft Tank (Rocket)
LCVP	Landing Craft Vehicle Personnel
LST	Landing Ship Tanks
Leutnant	German rank of Second Lieutenant
Lt	Lieutenant
LZ	Landing Zone
Maj	Major

Med	Medical
NCDU	Naval Combat Demolition Unit
OB	*Oberbefehlshaber* (Commander-in-Chief)
Obergefreiter	German rank of Corporal
Oberst	German rank of Colonel
Oberstleutnant	German rank of Lieutenant-Colonel
OKW	*Oberkommando der Wehrmacht* (Armed Forces High Command)
OMC	Ordnance Maintenance Company
PAK	*Panzerabwehrkanone* (anti-tank gun)
PC	Pilot Craft
PFAB	Parachute Field Artillery Battalion
Pfc	Private First Class
PIR	Parachute Infantry Regiment
Pvt	Private
Qm	Quartermaster
Reg	Regiment
RCT	Regimental Combat Team
Schütze	German rank of Private
Serv	Service
SETF	Special Engineer Task Force
SHAEF	Supreme Headquarters Allied Expeditionary Force
Sig Coy	Signal Company
SP	Self Propelled
T/4	Technician 4th Grade
TCC	Troop Carrier Command
TCG	Troop Carrier Group
TCW	Troop Carrier Wing
TF	Task Force
Trk	Truck
Trp	Troop
U-boat	German Submarine
USAAF	United States Army Air Force
VLA	Very Low Altitude
WIA	Wounded in Action

CHAPTER ONE

ALLIED FORCES AND PLANNING

The Overall Plan

In January 1944 General Dwight D. Eisenhower made a return visit to London, England. On this trip he had the four stars of a full general and the title of Commander of the Supreme Headquarters, Allied Expeditionary Force (SHAEF). Eisenhower's task was described to him in a directive from the Combined Chiefs of Staff. The instructions were succinct and the objective made very clear.

General Dwight D. Eisenhower, January, 1944.

> Its significant paragraph read: 'You will enter the continent of Europe and, in conjunction with the other Allied nations, undertake operations aimed at the heart of Germany and the destruction of her Armed Forces.' This purpose of destroying enemy forces was always our guiding principle.[1]

General Dwight D. Eisenhower, Supreme Commander, SHEAF.

The idea of a cross-channel invasion to France had been conceived and developed back in 1941. However, with operations in North Africa, the Far East and the Mediterranean taking up much of the resources and manpower it was later decided that such an offensive in northern France would not be feasible before 1944.

Codenamed Operation 'Overlord' the invasion of France was the largest and most complex combined operation ever to be attempted. In the final plans it was decided that the invasion would take place along a fifty mile stretch of the Normandy coastline from Ouistreham, at the mouth of the River Orne and Caen Canal in the east, to Quineville, on the Cotentin Peninsular in the west (see Map 1).

The initial seaborne assault of the invasion force, involving six divisions, would make

Cloth insignia of the Supreme Headquarters, Allied Expeditionary Force.

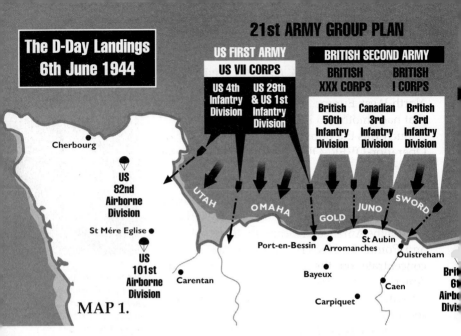

The D-Day Landings 6th June 1944

21st ARMY GROUP PLAN

US FIRST ARMY

US VII CORPS

US 4th Infantry Division

US 29th & US 1st Infantry Division

BRITISH SECOND ARMY

BRITISH XXX CORPS

BRITISH I CORPS

British 50th Infantry Division

Canadian 3rd Infantry Division

British 3rd Infantry Division

Cherbourg

US 82nd Airborne Division

St Mére Eglise

US 101st Airborne Division

Carentan

UTAH

OMAHA

GOLD

JUNO

SWORD

Port-en-Bessin

Arromanches

St Aubin

Ouistreham

Bayeux

Caen

Carpiquet

Brit 6t Airbo Divis

MAP 1.

their landings on five beaches codenamed 'Utah' and 'Omaha', for the Americans,[2] 'Sword' and 'Gold' for the British,[3] and 'Juno' for the Canadian Forces. Each nation putting its troops ashore at 0630 hrs, 0725 hrs and 0750 hrs, respectively, on Monday 5 June, 1944.

To protect both flanks of the seaborne invasion force, help destroy German strongpoints, and secure vital strategic points on the mainland, three Airborne divisions were also to be deployed in the early hours of D-Day, an assault that would take place prior to the seaborne invasion. The airborne forces were made up of the British 6th Airborne Division who would land in the east between the Caen Canal and River Dives,[4] (near Sword Beach), and the 82nd and 101st Airborne Division who would land on the Cotentin Peninsular (near Utah Beach).

The combined objective of the initial assault forces into Normandy was to establish and secure a bridgehead so that reinforcements could be brought ashore over the beaches. Due to the inclement weather Eisenhower was forced to postpone the operation for twenty-four hours, until the 6 June, 1944. Only then, in weather conditions that were still below the level that had been previously considered as acceptable for a successful landing, was the invasion of France to begin. Within the next six days of the operation the Allies would bring ashore some 326,547 men, 54,186 vehicles and 104,428 tons of stores into

Normandy[5] and slowly the tide would turn against the Nazis in the campaign to free North-West Europe of the oppressive regime that had smothered it for the past four years.

Such was the importance and complexity of Operation OVERLORD that other books in the *Battleground Europe Series* will cover each aspect of the landings in more concentrated detail; works covering the British and Canadian airborne and seaborne landings as well as the American landings at Omaha Beach and Pointe du Hoc. This book, however, will concentrate on the airborne assault by the American 82nd and 101st Airborne Divisions (around St Mère Église and Carentan) and the seaborne invasion on Utah Beach by the 4th US Infantry Division (with elements of the 90th Infantry Division) on the western flank of the invasion force on D-Day 6 June 1944.

The 'All-American' insignia of the 82nd American Airborne division. So named as a result of the division being made up of men from all the American states.

The Airborne Divisions

The first American assault forces into Normandy, on D-Day, were men from the 82nd (All American) and 101st (Screaming Eagles) Airborne Division. The 82nd Division was originally an infantry division which had formed on 25 August, 1917. It experienced sixty-eight days of combat in the First World War and suffered some 8,077 casualties during the Lorraine, Saint-Mihieland Meuse-Argonne offensives. The division was officially deactivated, after the Armistice, on 27 May, 1919 and was not activated again until the 25 March, 1942, under the command of, the then Brigadier-General, Omar N. Bradley[6].

It was during the early years of the Second World War that the idea of taking combat

The 'Screaming Eagles' insignia of the 101st American Airborne Division.

troops into battle by parachute or glider was developed. By the Summer of 1942 the British had formed the 1st Airborne Division and the Glider Pilot Regiment, both of which formed part of the Army Air Corps.

However, the Americans had not remained idle prior to their entrance into the war. As early as June, 1940, Major William 'Bill' Lee had been ordered to raise an airborne unit with volunteers from the 29th Infantry Division. By March, 1941, this unit became the 501st Parachute Infantry Battalion and other battalions were quickly formed soon afterwards, namely the 502nd, 503rd and 504th.

It was not until after the Japanese bombing of Pearl Harbour on 7 December, that same year, (when America and Japan declared war on each other and Hitler and Mussolini declared war on America) that the Second World War became truly global and America activated its war machine.

It was soon decided that the American Parachute Infantry Battalions needed to be increased in size and become regiments. Major 'Bill' Lee rose quickly through the ranks of the Army until, by June, 1942, he had become a one-star General.

In the last week of June, 1942, Brigadier-General Lee visited England with the then head of US Forces in the European Theatre of Operations, Major-General Eisenhower (soon to be promoted to Lieutenant-General on 7 July), USAAF commander Lieutenant-General Henry H. Arnold, and US supply chief Lieutenant-General Brehon B. Somerville. The reason for the visit was to see how America could best contribute to opening a second front in Europe. In addition they also went to exchange views with Britain's foremost Airborne operations theorist, and commander of the British 1st Airborne Division, Major-General F.A.M. 'Boy' Browning[7]. On his return to the US Brigadier-General Lee recommended the formation of an airborne division which would incorporate, in addition to the combat troops, engineers, artillery, signals and service units.

Meanwhile, Major-General Matthew B. Ridgeway had been appointed Commanding General (CG) of 82nd Infantry/ Motorised Division, in June, 1942. Bradley, having just been promoted to Major-General, was moved to take command of the 82nd Infantry Division. On 15 August, 1942 the War Department changed the division's name to 'Airborne' and the 82nd 'All-American'Airborne Division was officially born. In October, later that year, the division moved to its permanent home base at Fort Bragg.

Major-General Ridgeway was a respected professional soldier but had never made a parachute jump until after assuming command of the 82nd. Only then, with just ten minutes training, he made his first descent from a Dakota C-47 without any problems (though he did suffer a few bruises as a result of the rough, and fast, backward landing). He also became one of the first men of his division to travel in a Waco glider. This experience though proved somewhat more hazardous. During his landing his pilot told him to bale out of the door while the glider was still travelling at about 20 mph. An action that was necessary because the pilot had made his descent too quickly and the glider, having overshot the landing strip, was on a direct collision course for a parked USAAF bomber.[8] Along with the 82nd Airborne Division another new airborne division was also created, using a cadre from the 82nd, and named the 101st Airborne Division. This division adopted the distinctive insignia that latter gave rise to their nickname, the 'Screaming Eagles'. Brigadier-General Lee assumed command of the 101st from the start and was also promoted to Major-General. In a stirring inaugural address to his men the airborne innovator appealed to the Americans' sense of manifest destiny and spirit of adventure,

The 101st Airborne has no history, but it has a rendezvous with destiny. Like the early American pioneers, whose invincible courage was the foundation stone of this nation, we have broken with the past and its traditions in order to establish our claim to the future. Major-General William C. Lee, CG, 101st Airborne Division.

Tactical training in the early days was initially based upon the technique that German airborne troops had used during operations on Crete and at Fort Eben Emael. This involved using gliderborne troops in the initial attack and then, as was the case on Crete, reinforcements by parachute*.

However, a new strategy was later adopted by the division tacticians which involved deploying the paratroopers first and then using the gliderborne troops as reinforcements. A technique that would not be put fully to the test until June, 1944, in Operation OVERLORD.

On 9 July, 1943, eleven months after its formation, elements of the 82nd Airborne Division went into combat, at night, during Operation HUSKY; the invasion of Sicily.

This Sicilian operation, however, proved to be an omen and highlighted the difficulties and dangers of attempting airborne

*These were tactics that would serve the British 6th Airborne Division well during the Normandy Campaign in their capture of Pegasus Bridge.

operations in darkness while under enemy fire*. The first waves of paratroopers in Sicily had been widely scattered into enemy territory, leaving many troopers having to fight their own battles as individuals or small groups, and only a few were able to assemble and fight along the lines of the original battle plan.

Between September, 1943, and February, 1944, the 82nd and 101st Airborne Divisions were moved to England, encamped in the Midlands and Southern Regions, and prepared for the Allied invasion of North-West Europe. By this time the 82nd had seen its share of action during the Sicilian and Italian campaigns. The 101st, however, was yet untried and had yet to experience the brutal and unforgiving reality of battle. Nevertheless, all of the Parachute Infantry Regiments (PIR), whether combat experienced or not, had all received arduous and rigorous training before their transfer to England.

At no time was a trooper allowed to sit down, lean against anything or stand in a resting attitude when he was outside the confines of his own barracks. Another thing... was that at no time was a trooper allowed to walk from one point to another, unless ordered to do so; he must run or double-time.'9

Private Donald R. Burgett, 506th PIR, 101st A/B Division

While in England the 101st suffered a temporary set-back when Major-General Lee suffered a heart-attack and was forced to relinquish his command. His post was then filled by battle experienced Major-General Maxwell D. Taylor, the suave intellectual who had commanded the 82nd's artillery and distinguished himself as a result of his actions in Sicily and Italy. Despite his work in developing airborne warfare he was aware of the dangers and freely admitted to a dislike for jumping from airplanes, however, he was always quick to add that he liked associating with the men who did.[10]

The Seaborne Divisions

It was the American seaborne forces at Utah Beach that would be given the honour of becoming the first major Allied force to land on the beaches of Normandy on D-Day. Leading the assault force would be the men of the 4th (Ivy League) Infantry Division, though there would also be a battalion from the 359th Regiment, from the US 90th (Tough Ombres) Infantry Division,

*Though during Operation HUSKY, twenty-three planes, many fully laden with Paratroopers, were also shot down by 'friendly' anti-aircraft fire from US forces.

attached for the D-Day landings.

The 4th Infantry Division is one of America's regular army divisions and was formed during the First World War on the 3 December, 1917. The division had experienced some sixty-nine days of combat during the Aisne-Marne and Meuse-Argonne Campaigns – where the division suffered most of its 12,820 casualties – as well as some limited fighting in the Toul sector of the Saint-Mihiel Campaign. After the Armistice the division became part of the Army of Occupation in Germany until it was eventually deactivated in September, 1921.[11]

The 'Ivy League' insignia of the 4th Infantry Division. Ivy leaves were chosen as the symbol because ivy contains the roman numerals representing four in its first two letters (IV).

On 3 June, 1940, the 4th Infantry Division was reconstituted, under the command of Major General Walter E. Prosser, as America geared up its armed forces as a result of the increasing conflict on the European continent. The division went through a quick succession of commanders until, in July, 1942, Major-General Raymond O. Barton finally assumed command.

In addition to its regular training schedule the division also received amphibious training in the sunshine state of Florida before it was eventually sent overseas to Great Britain in January, 1944. While in the United Kingdom the men of the 4th Infantry Division prepared for their first active combat role in the Second World War, the Normandy landings.

The 4th Infantry Division was made up of three infantry regiments, the 8th, 12th and 22nd, commanded by Colonel James A. Van Fleet, Colonel Russel P. Reeder and Colonel Harvey A. Tribolet, respectively. In addition to these commanders the 4th Infantry Division also had the combat-experienced Brigadier General Theodore Roosevelt, Jr., the eldest son of the 26th President of the United States (and also cousin of the then 32nd President, F.D. Roosevelt), as Assistant Divisional Commander (ADC).

The 90th Infantry Division, activated on the 25 March, 1942, also went into combat for the first time on the beaches of Normandy, though only one battalion of the 359th Regiment was to land on D-Day. The remainder of the regiment and the rest of the 90th Infantry Division, were to follow on D+1. Further reinforcements, made up from the 9th Infantry Division, would begin landing on D+4 and were to assist in the capture of Cherbourg.[12]

Planning

The plans for Operation 'Overlord' were continually being analyzed and changed, during the build up to the invasion, as a result of the continuous flow of information that was being fed to the Allied commanders through the various intelligence-gathering systems. Detailed knowledge of the Normandy terrain and coastline, combined with an increasing understanding of how the Germans had utilised natural defences and established their own fortifications in the form of the formidable *Festung Europa* (aka. Atlantic Wall), helped the Allied planners anticipate and pin-point German troop deployments in the region.

The 'Tough Ombres' insignia of the 90th Infantry Division. The monogram of T&O represents the states of Texas and Oklahoma from which the Division was recruited. 'Tough Ombres' is merely a corruption of the Spanish for tough men.

In 1943 Lieutenant-General Frederick Morgan had been appointed Chief of Staff to the Supreme Allied Commander, also known as COSSAC (an acronym that became synonymous with his Anglo-American staff). It was the role of COSSAC to undertake a feasibility study and prepare the initial plans for a cross-channel invasion. It was during this time that Normandy was decided upon as the place where the Allied attack should take place.

The COSSAC plan, codenamed Operation 'Overlord' - for the overall plan - was presented to General Montgomery in January, 1944. General Montgomery had recently been appointed Commander-in-Chief of the 21st Army Group, and as such was in command of all Allied ground forces for 'Overlord.' The 21st Army Group comprised of the British Second Army, commanded by Lieutenant-General Miles Dempsey, and the US First Army, commanded by, the former 82nd Infantry Division Commander, Lieutenant-General Omar Bradley. The initial COSSAC plan involved the landing of only three seaborne divisions, on three beaches, onto a stretch of Normandy coastline only 25 miles wide. In addition, there were to be only two airborne brigades used in the initial assault. General Montgomery was quick to point out the logistical and tactical problems that would be faced in trying to reinforce such a narrow bridgehead, assuming, of course, that the relatively small force could actually establish a firm hold on the continent in the first place.

It was quickly decided that this plan needed to be expanded and so the beach area was doubled. This led to the inclusion of two more beaches 'Sword' and 'Utah'. Thus insuring that more troops could be

Cloth insignia of The First Army.

incorporated into the initial assault, on a broader front, and thereby weakening the inevitable counter-attacks from the Germans as their reinforcements would need to be displaced over a wider area.

It had first been envisaged that Operation 'Overlord' would take place on 1 May, 1944, in conjunction with another seaborne assault in Southern France, codenamed Operation 'Anvil'. The desired effect being that the Germans would have to split the reinforcements between the north and south of France. However, the Commander-in-Chief of the Naval Forces, Admiral Sir Bertram Ramsay, reported that the Admiralty were unsure if they were even able to meet the requirement of 3,323 landing craft and ships, 467 warships, and 150 minesweepers that would be needed for the COSSAC plan; and that was not considering the extra 240 warships, 1000 landing craft and extra 100 or so minesweepers that would now be needed to make the revised plan possible.[13]

With a series of logistical and material problems hampering the build-up it was decided that Operation 'Anvil' would be postponed until after the Normandy landings and that Operation 'Overlord,' itself, would also be delayed until June, 1944.

The assault phase of Operation 'Overlord' was codenamed Operation 'Neptune' and was developed by General Montgomery, Air Chief Marshal Sir Trafford Leigh-Mallory, Commander-in-Chief of the Allied Air Forces, and Admiral Sir Bertram Ramsay in an initial joint plan. Problems, however, were not just restricted to naval considerations. Montgomery had proposed that at least two, if not three, airborne divisions should be dropped before the seaborne landings took place. For the American airborne troops this would ultimately mean that their area of operations would be on the Cotentin Peninsular to both secure the causeways across the flooded marshes inland from Utah Beach and block the main route to Cherbourg. Such an operation would serve two purposes: the first would be to prevent, or at least delay, German reinforcements from attacking the initial assault forces on Utah Beach. The second, would be to prevent the Germans from reinforcing the port at Cherbourg; which, if all went as planned, would be captured as soon as possible (it was hoped by D+8),[14] to help in the resupply of the Allied Expeditionary Force.

This proposal for the airborne operations came under strong criticism from Air Chief Marshal Sir Leigh-Mallory, who argued that the terrain was unsuitable for airborne operations and that the heavy anti-aircraft defences in the area could decimate the American airborne forces. To make his point clear he predicted that losses in personnel and aircraft might run as high as 75 or 80 per cent.[15] Though there would be a variety of causes for the American airborne losses during the landings Leigh-Mallory's words would later prove to have been prophetic for some of the American units.

General Montgomery, with the backing of Lieutenant-General Bradley, insisted that such a force was necessary if there was to be any chance of capturing Cherbourg early on in the Normandy Campaign. The final decision on the matter, however, rested with the head of SHAEF, General Eisenhower. By early February, General Eisenhower had decided that the American airborne operation would be implemented on the Cotentin and that their assault would coincide with the British airborne operation to the east. Air Chief Marshal Sir Leigh-Mallory, reluctantly agreed but recommended that the airborne troops should land in an area away from the Germans' main defences – so that the troops would have time to organize themselves before they were attacked – and that their flight path should not cross over Cherbourg where there was a heavy concentration of anti-aircraft batteries. In addition he also insisted that the American gliderborne troops should not land before dawn.

There was additional opposition from the US Army Chief-of-Staff, General Marshall, in Washington, who proposed an even bolder plan that had been suggested by General Henry Arnold. This plan involved dropping all four of the Allied airborne divisions into an area halfway between the landing beaches and Paris, near the River Seine, so that the airfields there could be captured and more infantry flown into the battle zone; thereby opening another front against the German forces.[16] This plan, however, was rejected by General Eisenhower, not least because it was anticipated that the Germans would concentrate their forces in trying to drive the Allies back into the sea before they could establish a firm bridgehead. The need for airborne divisions on both flanks of the invasion force was therefore essential.

The major problem that faced the commanders, with regard the airborne operations, was the availability of suitable aircraft and crews. It was a matter that remained unresolved until the end of April, 1944, only then was it possible to guarantee enough aircraft to drop the 82nd and 101st US Airborne Divisions and two-thirds of the British 6th Airborne Division simultaneously.

With less than two weeks to go before D-Day, intelligence reports showed that the recently formed German 91st Airlanding Division - an active unit of German mobile reserves - had moved into the area around St. Sauveur-le-Vicomte, the same area where, it had been decided, the 82nd Airborne Division would be deployed.

The two American airborne divisions (placed under the direct command of the First Army during the build-up to the operation) would, on landing in Normandy, come under the command of VII Corps. As a result of this the two airborne commanders, Major-Generals Ridgeway and Taylor, were able to receive their battle plans direct from the First Army Staff, but also had the benefit of close collaboration with VII Corps Commander Major-General Joseph Lawton Collins.[17] At Lieutenant-General Bradley's Head-quarters, in Bristol, on 27 May, 1944, the plans were once again scrutinized. With only nine days left before the invasion,

The cloth insignia of VII Corps.

the final operational plans and objectives were decided upon for the 82nd and 101st Airborne Divisions.

In addition to the actual planning of the assault itself there were also a series of deception plans implemented. One such operation, 'Fortitude,' was taking place as the planners decided on their final plans for Operation 'Overlord'. Part of Operation 'Fortitude' involved bombing campaigns and operations of the Allied Expeditionary Air Force (made up of RAF Bomber Command, US Strategic Air Forces and the Tactical Air Forces) which were carried out across the whole of Northern France. The intention of these raids was to distract the Germans' attention from the planned assault areas and, by putting an emphasis on the attacks in the Pas-de-Calais area, it was hoped that the German High Command could be convinced that the cross-channel invasion would take place across the narrowest point of the English Channel.

The British Second Tactical Air Force and US Ninth Air Force made up the Tactical Air Forces and came under the Command of Air Chief Marshal Leigh-Mallory. Beginning their operations many weeks before D-Day it was the task of these forces to disrupt the German flow of supplies and reinforcements to the front, by destroying the enemy's railway and road networks. There was also the need to attack all the airfields within a 130 mile radius of the Normandy beaches to reduce the amount of air cover that the enemy would

Cloth insignia of 9th Air Force

have when the invasion began. Most importantly though, by destroying the bridges over the River Seine and River Loire, the Tactical Air Forces would be able to effectively isolate the area near the landing beaches from the rest of France.

During the invasion itself the Tactical Air Forces would also be deployed in a variety of tasks. These ranged from providing escort protection (for the Strategic Air Forces as they went on bombing raids and for the Airborne troops as they were transported to their drop and landing zones) to giving air cover for the naval forces as they approached the landing beaches and for the seaborne troops as they disembarked. Finally, in an offensive role during the campaign, they would be used to destroy enemy targets such as gun emplacements, armoured columns and fuel dumps. In addition the pilots were also tasked with delaying any German reinforcements they saw from being moved to the front line.

The Strategic Air Forces, by D-Day, were made up of both RAF Bomber Command and the US Strategic Air Forces, commanded by Air Chief Marshal Sir Arthur 'Bomber' Harris and Lieutenant-General Carl A. Spaatz respectively. While their bombing raids concentrated attacks on the German transportation and communication systems, they were also used to cripple the German armament and supply industry by bombing factories and oil refineries in the Ruhr; Germany's industrial production centre.

The operations of the Strategic and Tactical Air Forces of the Allied Expeditionary Air Force were co-ordinated by the senior Allied airman, Air Chief Marshal Sir Arthur Tedder, who had also by this time been appointed Eisenhower's second in command and been given the title of Deputy Commander of the Supreme Headquarters, Allied Expeditionary Force.

Air Raids

As D-Day approached it had become clear that Germany's capability to reinforce itself had been severely affected by the sustained and devastating air attacks of the Allied Expeditionary Air Force. Credit must also be given to the brave French resistance workers who, in conjunction with the British Special Operations Executive, helped identify potential targets and cause disruption by destroying or sabotaging vital railway links and communication lines.

By the time of the invasion seventy-four of the Bridges and tunnels, leading to the Normandy assault beaches, had been destroyed or made impassable. In addition, much of the German communication and supply infrastructure was in chaos as a result of the shortage of rolling stock, fuel, and adequate repair facilities.[18] The final massive blow by the Allied Expeditionary Air Force, however, would begin on the eve of the invasion and last throughout the night. During that night Bomber Command would laydown its most intense bombing raid so far of the war, by dropping over 5,000 tons of bombs on the beach defences and coastal batteries along the Normandy coastline from Fontenay, in the east, to St-Martin-de-Varreville in the west.[19] Thereby helping to soften the German defences for the initial assault by the airborne and seaborne troops.

In the meantime, the massive Allied war machine was picking up momentum and as soon as Eisenhower made the decision to invade there would be no turning back. Responsibility for the success of the operation would then rest in the collective action of each individual soldier, sailor and airman. The logistics and intricate assault plans would then be put fully to the test by the combat troops during the first 24 hours; it would be a test that would not only decide the outcome for the Battle of Normandy, but ultimately the course of the Second World War.

1. Eisenhower, Dwight D. *Crusade in Europe*. (William Heinemann Ltd., London, 1948). p.247.

2. See *Omaha Beach* by Tim Kilvert Jones. *Battleground Europe Series*.

3. See *Sword Beach* by Tim Kilvert Jones & *Gold Beach* by Christopher Dunphie. *Battleground Europe Series*.

4. See *Pegasus Bridge/Merville Battery*, by Carl Shilleto, *Battleground Europe Series*.

5. Report by The Supreme Commander to the Combined Chiefs of Staff on the Operations in Europe. (H.M.S.O. London, 1946). p.32. (referred to hereafter as *The Eisenhower Report*).

6. Jacobs, Bruce. *Soldiers, Fighting Divisions of the Regular Army*, (W.W. Norton & Company Inc., New York, 1958). p.251-263.

7. Gregory, Barry & John Bachelor. *Airborne Warfare 1918-1945*. (Phoebus Publishing Company, London, 1979). pp.68-72.'

8. Crookenden, Napier. *Dropzone Normandy*. (Ian Allan Ltd, Shepperton, 1976). p.20.

9. Katcher, Philip. *US 101st Airborne Division 1942-1945*. (Osprey Publishing Ltd, London, 1978). p.4.

10. Boatner III, Mark M. *Biographical Dictionary of World War II*. (Presido Press, Navato, 1996). p.555.

11. op. cit. Jacobs, Bruce. pp.96-113.

12. Compiled from information in the Department of The Army, Historical Division, publication: *Utah Beach To Cherbourg (6th June – 27th June 1944)* available from the Superintendent of Documents, U.S. Government Printing Office Washington, D.C., 20402. (referred to hereafter as *Beach to Cherbourg Report*). pp.10 & 55.

13. Wilmot, Chester. *The Struggle For Europe*, (Reprint Society Ltd, 1954). p.189. for a detailed breakdown of naval warships used see: Edwards, Commander Kenneth, *Operation Neptune*. (Collins, London, 1946). p.39-51.

14. op. cit. *The Eisenhower Report* p.9.

15. op. cit. Wilmot, Chester. p.188.

16. op. cit. Crookenden, Napier. p.67.

17. op. cit. *Utah Beach to Cherbourg Report* p.9.

18. op. cit. *The Eisenhower Report*. p.21.

19. Middlebrook & Everitt, *The Bomber Command War Diaries* (Midland Publishing Ltd., Leics., 1996). p.523.

CHAPTER TWO

DISASTER BEFORE D-DAY

Exercise Tiger

With the time for the invasion of Normandy moving closer it was decided by the Allied commanders, in February, 1944, that major, full scale rehearsals of the Normandy landings should take place. Rehearsals that would serve not only to see how well the planners had organised the details and logistics of the planned invasion, but also give the troops and commanders some experience of making a seaborne and airborne assault.

The commanders of the British Second Army and US First Army, Lt-Gen Sir Miles Dempsey and Lt-Gen Omar Bradley, respectively, received orders in the form of the Initial Joint Plan for Operation NEPTUNE (the codename given to the assault phase of Operation OVERLORD), orders which asked for each commander to submit detailed plans for the landing of the two Allied Armies in Normandy.

Amongst the intricate plans, detailing the operations of the combined forces of the navy, airforce and army, the US First Army submitted details of a dress rehearsal for VII Corps. Amongst these plans was an exercise for the Utah Beach landings. This rehearsal was scheduled for April and would take place in an area of South Hams, in Devon, known as Slapton Sands.[1]

Slapton Sands had been chosen by the military as a training area because of its marked resemblance to the stretch of

Slapton Sands.

coastline on the Cotentin Peninsular which would soon come to be known as 'Utah' Beach. The long stretch of beach at Slapton Sands was separated from the mainland by a lake and marshland with two bridges that provided access to and from the beach. This was terrain very similar to the natural causeways that went through the flooded marshland near Utah Beach.

Back in November, 1943, the local population of an area covering some 30,000 acres, including the villages of Blackawton, Chillington, East Allington, Sherford, Slapton, Stokenham, Strete and Torcross, had been informed that their land and property were to be requisitioned under the *1939 Defence Regulations and Compensation Act*.[2]

It was to be a massive undertaking, and in the space of only six weeks 3,000 civilians, and their possessions, were evacuated and rehoused to make way for the 30,000 US troops that were deployed and encamped in the area.

The evacuation of the local population was necessary not just because of the secrecy that needed to be maintained around the military exercises, but also for the civilians' own protection. This was because some of the exercises which had been planned, would be no soft dummy run for the troops that were participating. Instead the exercises would be a realistic simulation of battle conditions, which would include a naval and aerial bombardment and the use of live ammunition by the troops.

Naturally, all the live ammunition being fired in the exercise would be fired above the heads of the assault troops, however, it has been alleged that communication problems, during the early exercises, meant that some of the troops did not know that they were using live ammunition.

The order for live ammunition to be used had come from the top, from General Eisenhower himself, the intention being that its use would toughen the troops and commanders, thereby better preparing them for the hardship of real battle.

However, although this order was passed down the chain of command, it has been said that the order never reached all the troops that were taking part in the exercise. In addition, it has also been stated that incorrect radio frequencies had been given to the commanding officers and marshals who were to coordinate the exercise between the attacking troops, on board

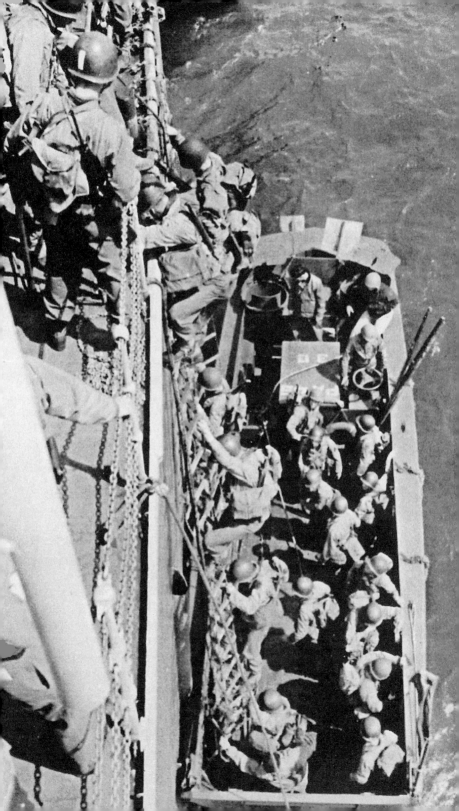

naval vessels at sea, and the troops who were defending on the shore. In the event, this meant that the vital communication system needed to coordinate the various units of the landing forces were useless and that in the resulting confusion casualties occurred as men were hit by live ammunition.

Reports of men being killed and wounded have come from eyewitness accounts made by veterans who took part in the dress rehearsal landings at Slapton Sands. Though, today, there is no documentary evidence from official sources to substantiate these claims.

Where there is plenty of official evidence though, with regards to one tragedy surrounding the pre-invasion rehearsals, is in the operational records of Exercise 'Tiger'.

In this exercise there were a number of communication problems between the Landing Ship Tanks (LSTs) and their naval protection escorts. In the follow-up convoy for Exercise 'Tiger,' which was to land on the 28th August, the LST's had been given radio frequencies that did not correspond with those used by the British Naval Headquarters or with HMS *Azalea*; a Royal Navy corvette that had been tasked with protecting the LST's as they made their way, from Portsmouth and Brixham, to their final destination at Slapton Sands (this has been attributed to typographical errors in the orders issued[3]).

In yet another error a second naval vessel, the destroyer HMS *Scimitar*, which had also been assigned to protect the convoy, was taken into port for repairs on the eve of the exercise and, as a result of a lost signal, no other vessel was sent in its place to escort and protect the convoy.[4]

The recipe for disaster was in the making. On the night of the 27 April, 1944, a convoy of five heavily laden LST's set off from Plymouth and met up with three other LST's that had departed from Brixham. Then, with only one ship for protection, the convoy began its ill-fated journey for Slapton Sands in Lyme Bay.

Further out to sea though, the Royal Navy was on heightened alert as a result of the exercise, a patrol of eight motor torpedo boats had been deployed off Cherbourg,[5] a main E-boat base for the Germans, in order to intercept any of the E-boat patrols that regularly reconnoitred the English Channel.

However, despite the extra surveillance by the Royal Navy a flotilla of nine* E-boats was still able to set out from Cherbourg,

* The actual number of E-boats involved varies, in primary and secondary sources, from seven to nine. Nine is the number officially recognised in the Operational Archives of the Naval Historical centre, Washington DC. USA.

unchallenged, on a course heading for Lyme Bay. The same area where the LST convoy was heading in preparation for the landing at Slapton Sands the following morning.

The LST Group was named Convoy T-4 and consisted of *USS LST's 515, 496, 511, 531, 58*, from Plymouth, and *USS LST's 499, 289 and 507* from Brixham. Once they had formed a single column the convoy made its way, at a rate of six knots, towards Slapton Sands in the same order that has just been listed.[6] Ahead of them went mine-clearing ships, sweeping the channel for enemy mines, just as they would need to do in the real invasion in only a few weeks.

Exercise 'Tiger' was spread over several days, from the 22-29 April, 1944.[7] Each day would then incorporate a number of various operational assignments for the troops. Missions that would have to be undertaken so that the exercise would be an accurate simulation of the real combined operation.

The actual beach landings for VII Corps were scheduled for the 27 and 28 April. This part of the operation began on the evening of the 26 April when the initial assault force, carrying elements of the 4th Infantry Division, began their seaborne journey to Slapton Sands. By the end of the following day this part of the exercise was completed, though not without some operational and communication problems. Despite these the difficulties were overcome and their was no interference from any German aircraft or boats.

The previous exercises in this area had also been undertaken

US Naval Beach Battalion on excercise at Slapton Sands.

LST 325 unloads on Slapton Sands on 22 January, 1944.

without any major difficulties. Back in January, Exercise 'Duck I', had taken place with V Corps, involving units from the 29th Infantry Division and the 1st Engineer Special Brigade that were to land at 'Omaha' Beach. This exercise, involving some 10,000 troops, and the following two exercises 'Duck II' and 'Duck III' (held in February), to help train the units not involved in the first exercise, taught the planners and troops valuable lessons.

The first exercises for the VII Corps, destined for Utah Beach landings began with Exercise 'Beaver'. Completed in March, this exercise also involved the airborne and seaborne units of the 101st Airborne Division (though the airborne units in this exercise were taken to their drop-zones by truck and not parachuted in[8]). Again many lessons were learnt during this exercise.

The next major rehearsal was Exercise 'Fox' which involved 17,000 troops of V Corps, and provided more practice for the Regimental Combat Teams that would storm the beach at 'Omaha'. Then in April, came the penultimate and most infamous rehearsal, Exercise 'Tiger.' This was a major dress rehearsal for the Utah Beach landings for VII Corp, and involved the 82nd and 101st Airborne division as well as the 4th Infantry Division and attached units.

The follow-up LST Group, Convoy T-6, carrying troops for

the beach build-up part of the exercise, made its journey across Lyme Bay at just after midnight on the night of the 27 April. At the same time a German flotilla of E-boats had also managed to reach Lyme Bay having successfully avoided the three British motor torpedo boats, two motor gun boats and four destroyers that were tasked with creating a defensive screen around the area.[9]

The E-boat flotilla, on reaching Lyme Bay, then split into two groups, with one covering the western side of the bay and the other the eastern side. Before long the E-boat commanders spotted the LST convoy. The sea that night was calm and the weather and visibility were fair, ideal conditions for the E-boats to operate in.

> *We approached the convoy from the northwest and had no problems attacking the rear of the convoy in view of our superior speed. We normally did 34 to 36 knots out of harbour, even when dropping mines. Only when firing torpedoes did we need to bring our speed down to around 10 knots. The high speed was needed to avoid radar plotting by escorts.*
> Oberleutnant Zur See Hans Schirren, Commanding Officer E-boat S-145

The German E-boats were a formidable foe for the relatively slow moving LST's, armed with twin torpedo tubes, and weapons that varied from 20mm to 40mm guns, they were propelled by powerful Daimler-Benz engines. Immediately upon sighting the convoy the E-boats went into action and launched their torpedoes at the LST's.

Most of the torpedoes initially missed the LST's, the shallow draft of the ships allowing the torpedoes to pass beneath them harmlessly. But not all the LST's were that fortunate. The first to

LST 507 crossing the Atlantic in March, 1944.

Kapitan Rudolf Petersen was the commander of the S-Boats (*Schnellboote)* and controlled operations in the Channel. For the attack on American transports during Exercise 'Tiger' he was awarded the Oak Leaves to his Iron Cross.

receive a direct hit was *LST 507*. The ship did not sink immediately but instead a raging fire, caused by the explosion of the torpedo, slowly began to take hold. Desperate efforts by the navy personnel to keep the fire under control proved to be in vain and after the ship had lost all its power the order to abandon ship was given.

It was an order that some had not waited for. As soon as some of the men witnessed the fire they decided that they would prefer to take their chances in the water. The LST's were packed with army and navy personnel, the majority of whom were from units of the US 1st Engineer Special Brigade; as it was these that would perform the beachhead build-up phase of the exercise.

When the men began to abandon ship another communication problem was to come to light and this time the consequences would prove fatal for many of the soldiers. The problem this time regarded the use of the life saving equipment issued to the army personnel. Though each man had been issued with an inflatable life preserver, nobody, it would seem, had bothered to issue any instructions on how they should be properly used.

The type of lifebelt issued to the army was designed to be worn around the upper part of the chest and underneath the armpits. However, because of the cumbersome equipment and backpacks worn by the soldiers, some found that the lifebelt could be worn more comfortably around their waist. Subsequently, when these men jumped into the water they found themselves to be top heavy. If they had not discarded their packs before jumping into the water they would find themselves floundering in the sea with the weight of their equipment holding their heads beneath the water. Another problem also arose when it was found that some of the soldiers had not been given proper instructions on how to inflate the life preservers, and in the event of having to use their life jackets they had to try and work out how to inflate them by themselves.

Some of the life rafts on *LST 507* were able to be released and slid into the water but, unfortunately, not all of them were put to sea. Within minutes the sea around the ship seemed to be full of bodies, some frantically trying to swim away from the burning ship while others lay motionless with no sign of life. Some of the men just jumped over the side unaware, or unconcerned, where they would land. Others tried to compose themselves, amid the chaos and confusion, before plunging into the dark freezing waters of the English Channel.

We had to go. We inflated our life jackets, held hands, [jumped and] *we hit the water. Boom! You go down, salt water, about 40 degrees, oh! Cold. Then we started to drift away. The water was on fire. All around us you could smell the oil and gas. Then you see the soldiers and hear their death cry in the water. Who was hit? Who had an arm and leg missing? As I looked up I saw a couple of sailors wrapped around a 40mm gun, their heads hanging..., blood, they were dead.*

Private First Class, P. J. Giacchi, 557th Quartermaster Railhead Company, 1st Engineer Special Brigade. LST 507.

The fire engulfed some of the soldiers and sailors in the water, while the rest of the men, some clinging to life rafts, kicked desperately in the water trying to get themselves away form the now listing LST and raging fire. For the sailors that survived there was also an added incentive to get away from the ship; because they knew that if the ship sank quickly then those in the immediate vicinity could face being sucked down into the sea as the vessel plunged to the bottom of the channel.

The night air was filled with the screams or cries of wounded or burning men. For those that had been fortunate to have survived the torpedo explosion, the 20ft plus jump into the water and the burning sea, there lay ahead another danger; the long and cold struggle for survival in the chilled water of the sea. For unknown to them it would be several hours before any attempts at rescue could be made.

The next ship to be hit by a torpedo was *LST 531*, which had engaged in a firefight with one or more of the E-boats. The first torpedo fired at the ship hit amidship on the starboard side and exploded creating a ball of flames. A minute later a second torpedo slammed into the side of the ship and within seconds the whole ship seemed to be ablaze. The engines stopped almost immediately on impact and the power and communication systems went down. Within minutes the ship began to list heavily. After another ten minutes *LST 531* had capsized and was sinking beneath the waves.

Other LST's began firing out to sea in the panic, but in the confusion and darkness some of the machine gun fire was hitting the other ships in the convoy and not the German E-boats. The night was illuminated with an assortment of colours as tracer fire (red and green from the Allied guns, red and yellow from the German guns) was shot into the air and sea during the battle.

At about 02.25 hrs emergency signals were sent from two of the LST's stating the convoy was under attack (initially, because of the torpedo impacts, it was thought that the convoy was under attack from German U-boats). However, the British warships nearest the area did not receive the messages as they were tuned into different frequencies.

In the meantime, the error of sending just one escort, HMS *Azalea*, with Convoy T-4 had just been realised by Plymouth Headquarters. At 01.30 hrs an order went out to HMS *Saladin* to go and join the convoy of LSTs. However, HMS *Saladin* was some thirty miles away from the convoy and would take at least an hour and a half to reach them.[10]

HMS *Azalea*, the small Flower-class corvette, with a top speed of about sixteen knots, was one mile ahead of the LST convoy as they made their way across Lyme Bay. When the thirty-five knot E-boats launched their attack against the convoy the corvette could do little to help. At about 02.30 hrs *LST 289* found itself under attack. As the gun crews fired at one of the E-boats the distinctive wake of a torpedo was seen heading towards the ship. Despite diversionary action by the ship's captain,

LST 289 off Slapton Sands.

Lieutenant Harry Mettler, the torpedo struck the starboard stern side of the ship. After the initial flash and explosion fires broke out in the crew's quarters and on the navigation bridge. Fortunately the fires were contained and were soon brought under control by the quick action of the naval crew. Though the torpedo had caused some severe damage, the engines were still operable and the ship was not completely crippled. Between 03.30 and 04.15 hrs the E-boat commanders decided to return to Cherbourg. On route they were intercepted by HMS *Orwell*. However, the E-boats were able to escape without any damage being inflicted on them. The E-boats were then placed under attack by British aircraft, which resulted in one of the German boats being hit, however the damage was not serious and all the craft eventually made it back to base without any losses.

HMS *Saladin* finally approached the stricken convoy, which by this time had resumed formation, at around 03.15 hrs. As they came across the area where the LST's had been sunk the crew spotted and began rescuing some of the survivors, some fifty of which were clinging to the bow of one of the sunken LST's that was still protruding above the water. After picking up just a few of the survivors the escort ship captain decided that he ought to begin searching for the E-boats in case any further attack was planned by the Germans.

LST 289 had, fortunately, managed to keep afloat during this time and the crew had also lowered and powered up some of the LCVP's that she was carrying to help steer and move the damaged ship. Some of the other remaining LST's were steered, under the protection of the HMS *Azalea*, towards West Bay and when they were close to the shore they weighed their anchor and waited for news of what was happening and what they should do next.

Major-General Joseph Lawton Collins VII Corps Commander.

Not until around 05.00 hrs did the search begin in earnest for more survivors. By this time *LST 515* had returned, lowered its boats into the sea, and was picking up what remained of the survivors. But with over two and a half hours of immersion in the bitterly cold sea, hypothermia had taken its toll amongst the soldiers and sailors and many had perished.

Because of communication problems, it wasn't until 06.25 hrs that Rear-Admiral Don P. Moon, the Naval commanding officer of the exercise, was informed of the attack[11] while aboard his command ship USS *Bayfield*. Immediately he ordered further rescue ships to the area and started an investigation into the matter.

Rear-Admiral Don P.Moon Task Force 'U' Commander.

Throughout the day the scale of the tragedy was slowly realized as only 317 men were rescued from the sea. The official total number of casualties, according to the naval action reports, was 639 (198 navy, 441 army). Army reports later put their dead and missing at 551, bringing the total to 749.[12] Of the three ships torpedoed *LST 289* suffered the least amount of casualties, with only thirteen killed and twenty-one wounded (most of whom were navy personnel). The remaining 736 dead and missing, were all from LST 507 and LST 531. The majority of these, some 268 men, were from 3206th Quartermaster Service Company and 557th Railhead Company, 1st Special Engineering Brigade.[13]

In total though, according to the figures compiled by the 1st Engineer Brigade after the war, the engineers lost 413 men in the disaster.

The loss of so many men was naturally a cause of great concern for the commanders and there was, many years after the war, talk of there having been an official cover-up on the disaster. It was news that generated a lot of media attention and subsequently the stories and hearsay were hyped up into a typical sensationalist media news item. True, in the weeks immediately after the event, things were officially hushed up. An action that can not be said to be unusual considering the actual invasion of France was still being prepared and was about to take place in less than six weeks. The last thing the commanders would have wanted at that time was for any news of a major disaster to leak out amongst the troops. The effect that such news may have had on morale could have been terrible. Besides, everything concerning the build-up for the invasion was top-secret, as all troop movement and preparation for D-Day had to be kept from German intelligence.

Three sources, that can undoubtedly put an end to any question of a post-war cover-up, and also end the media speculation of there having being a conspiracy of silence, they are: *Three Years With Eisenhower*, by Captain Harry C. Butcher (Eisenhower's Naval Aide), *Operation Neptune* by Commander Kenneth Edwards, Royal Navy, and *Top Secret*, by Ralph Ingersoll. Each of these three books were published in 1946, at a time when even the most trivial official War Office documentation was still classified, and all speak openly and frankly about the disaster:

> *There was the morning we woke up and heard that the E-boat... had got into a convoy of our big LSTs, sunk two and blew the stern off another, not ten mile from Portland Bill. Five or six hundred Americans were casualties, wounded or drowned out there in the dark.*[14]

        Major Ralph Ingersoll, Staff Officer, 21st Army Group.

As an intelligence officer, assigned to General Montgomery's Headquarters, Major Ingersoll received first hand accounts of the events during his investigation of the attack. No one can question his knowledge of the events and the fact that his work, and the work of other, high ranking, officers was able to be published so soon after the war speaks for itself and confirms that there was no post-war cover-up.

One might, quite rightly, assume that the loss of so many men would have caused the greatest and most concern amongst the Allied commanders. But not so. With the real invasion so near there were two other major problems left to sort out in the wake of the E-boat attack. The first problem was concerning the loss of the LST's, with so many troops having to be transported over to Normandy during the invasion landing craft were a scarce commodity and replacements would prove difficult to find. The second problem though was far more serious, and threatened not just to compromise the logistical plans of the invasion, but possibly the whole of Operation 'Overlord' itself.

The Missing Bigots

The most pressing problem for the Allied Commanders was the loss of the Bigots. Bigot was the name given to information of the highest classification. Any information, that may be of use to the enemy, was placed in a classification scale that went from

Practice landings on Slapton sands.

Restricted to *Confidential* to *Secret*. Above this there was the British classification of *Most Secret* which was on a par with the American *U.S. Secret*. Next came *Top Secret* and finally, with regards to Operation Overlord, there came *Bigot*.

What was so important about the Bigots was they were the men who were privy to detailed information that meant they knew the exact time and location of the forthcoming invasion. Unfortunately, for the Allied commanders, it was estimated that some ten Bigoted officers were missing after the German E-boat attack.[15] Major Ralph Ingersoll, as part of his investigation into the disaster, revealed to Montgomery's headquarters that it was quite possible that the Germans may have taken some prisoners during their attack. With this information it was imperative that a search begin for the bodies of the Bigots.

The problem now was the sheer number of men that were dead or missing, over 600. Immediately plans were put into action to start recovering as many of the bodies as possible, action which included sending divers down to search the wrecks of the LSTs, and patrol boats to search the sea and shoreline. In the meantime the Allied commanders could only wait and consider the alternatives of what might happen next; if one of the Bigots had fallen into the hands of the Germans Operation OVERLORD may have been compromised. It was a thought almost too bitter to contemplate. If, however, the bodies of the Bigots were not recovered the Allies were still faced with a very limited number of options. Either cancel the operation and begin preparations for another or wait and see if the Germans began redeploying their troops and Panzer Divisions to positions that would indicate they knew the Allied plans and objectives. If that did happen then the planners would still have to start all over again.

Amazingly, all the bodies of the Bigoted officers were recovered and accounted for. Considering that over 250 bodies were never found from the sunken LSTs the discovery of the Bigots was nothing short of a miracle. With this news SHAEF could breath a sigh of relief and continue with the process of training and equipping the Allied forces in preparation for the invasion.

Final Exercises

The rehearsals still continued after Exercise 'Tiger.' In May Exercise 'Fabius', involving 25,000 troops destined for Omaha Beach, began at the start of the month. This time there was no interference from German E-boats. The American airborne units also continued their training, culminating in a full-scale dress rehearsal for the 101st Airborne Division when it was dropped on the Berkshire Downs. The resulting assessment of the airborne drop was put at 75 per cent successful, despite some twenty-eight aircraft having to return to base with full loads as they couldn't locate their drop zone. But the airborne drops were not without their own incidents though, and as a result of that exercise the 101st suffered some 436 casualties.[16]

Despite the misfortunes experienced during the training programme, valuable lessons were learnt as the planners and organisers assessed and evaluated the complex series of exercises. Not all the assessments were favourable though and some of the commanders were quite displeased with the way some units and men behaved and performed. General Eisenhower's Naval Aide went so far as to express his grave doubts about the ability of the troops when he witnessed part of Exercise 'Tiger' in April.

I am particularly concerned over the absence of toughness and alertness of the young American officers whom I saw on this trip. They seem to regard war as one grand manoeuvre in which they are having a happy time. Many seem as green as growing corn. How will they act in battle and how will they look in three

Practice landings continued into the month of May.

*months' time?... A good many of the colonels also give me a pain.
They are fat, grey and oldish. Most of them wear the rainbow
ribbon of the last war and are still fighting it.'*[17]
Captain Harry C. Butcher, Naval Aide to General Dwight D. Eisenhower.

The combination of mishaps and problems that blighted the
exercises for the Utah Beach and airborne landings, must also
have left a lasting impression on those that knew about the
tragedies first hand. The sense of trepidation about what lay
ahead must have been particularly acute, especially for those
survivors of Convoy T-4 who had to embark upon another
sailing aboard a LST.

The thought that must have passed through the minds of
those young men of what the real invasion would be like,
having now experienced and considered the casualties
sustained in the practice invasion, is one which is almost
beyond comprehension.

The only consolation that was available for those that
survived the horrors of being torpedoed, or having experienced
some mishap during a parachute decent, was that their wait

wouldn't be a long one. For within a few weeks those soldiers, sailors and airmen would be aboard their transport and heading towards the coastline of Normandy into a real battle.

1. US First Army Operations Plan for 'Neptune', dated February, 1944.
2. Small, Ken. *The Forgotten Dead* (Bloomsbury Publishing Ltd., London, 1993). p.7.
3. MacDonald, Charles B. Article *Slapton Sands; The Cover-up That Never Was'* extracted from *Army 38, No. 6, June, 1988,* p.64. Published by the Department of the Navy, Naval Historical Center, Washington DC.
4. Berger, Sid. *Breaching Fortress Europe* (Kendall/Hunt Publishing Company, Dubuque, Iowa (USA). 1994). p.94.
5. Hoyt, Edwin P. *The Invasion Before Normandy* (Robert Hale Ltd., London, 1988). p.101.
6. Document titled *Operation Tiger* published by the Department of the Navy, Operational Archives, Naval Historical Center, Washington DC, Aug., 1996.
7. Operational Orders for Exercise 'Tiger,' classified *Top Secret*, issued 19 April, 1944 by the Supreme Headquarters of the Allied Expeditionary Force.
8. op. cit. Crookenden, Napier. p.29.
9. op.cit. Hoyt, Edwin P. p.101.
10. ibid. p.103.
11. ibid. p.115.
12. op. cit. Document titled *'Operation Tiger'*.
13. Devoe, Howard G. *History of the 1st Engineer Amphibian Brigade and the 531st Engineer Shore Regiment and Succeeding Units.* Private publication for 531st Engineer Association, 1983. Library of Congress Card No. 83-173453. p.15.
14. Ingersoll, Ralph. *Top Secret.* (Partridge Publications, Ltd., London, 1946). p.82.
15. ibid. p.84.
16. op. cit. Crookenden, Napier. p.29.
17. Butcher, Harry C. *Three Years With Eisenhower.* (William Heinemann Ltd., London, 1946). pp.454-455.

View from inside a German casemate housing a 24 cm gun at St Marcouf.

CHAPTER THREE

ALLIED OBJECTIVES & GERMAN DEFENCES

Pathfinders

The first American airborne troops into Normandy would be the Pathfinder teams. Made up from men of both the 82nd and 101st Airborne Divisions they were due to land around 00.15 hrs on D-Day. The Pathfinders were split into eighteen groups, with three groups assigned to each of the six drop zones (three for the 101st and three for the 82nd Airborne Division drop zones). To mark the drop zones effectively the Pathfinders were equipped with *'Eureka'* radar transmitter and receiver beacons, these British-designed and American-made beacons were carried by the paratroopers and would be set up on each of the designated drop zones. The Pathfinders were under orders not to activate their transmitters until fifteen minutes before the following aircraft, carrying the assault forces, were due to pass overhead.

The leading aircraft of the assault formations were equipped with a corresponding radar receiver and transmitter known as *'Rebecca'*. By setting the *'Eureka'* and *'Rebecca'* beacons to different frequencies the aircraft were able to distinguish between the different drop zones.

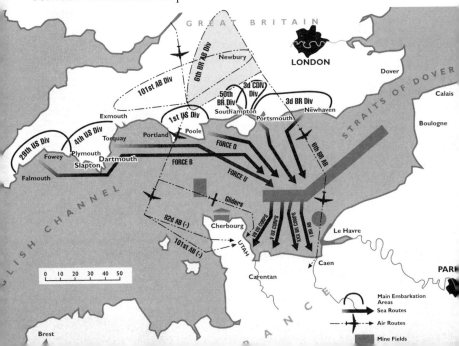

In addition to the *'Eureka'* and *'Rebecca'* beacons there were two other forms of electronic tracking and location devices. The first was the British *'GEE'* radio system which was designed to receive three separate radio pulses, transmitted from bases back in England and with the use of a specially prepared grid map the navigators were able to use triangulation to determine their exact position. The second form of tracking device was the American *'SCR-717'* which was an early form of scanner that provided a crude map of the area below an aircraft on a radar screen. Used in conjunction with a responder unit, called *'BUPS'*, that were given to the Pathfinders, the unit, when activated, would produce a bright spot on the aircraft navigator's *'SCR-717'* radar screen thereby giving the units location in proximity to the aircraft.[1]

Finally, there were also visual aids in the form of 'Holophane' and 'Krypton' lights[2] which were laid out in a 'T' shape and gave the incoming pilots, if weather permitted, a visual point of reference. Throughout the drop there was to be no radio voice contact between the airborne troops and aircraft crews. In addition, flares were only to be used by the various unit commanders in helping their men assemble after the drop.

101st Airborne Division

The 101st Airborne Division in Operation 'Albany' were the next to drop into Normandy at approximately 01.00 hrs (H-5 hrs), about one hour after the Pathfinders (for full Order of Battle see Appendix A). The 502nd PIR and 377th Parachute Field Artillery Battalion were due to land at Drop Zone 'A', between Turqueville and St-Martin-de-Varreville; the 1/506th, 2/506th and 3/501st PIR were to land north of Hiesville, and north-east of St-Marie-du-Mont, on Drop Zone 'C'; and 1/501st, 1/502nd and 3/506th PIR, with the Divisional Commander Major-General Taylor, were to land south of Vierville, and northeast of St-Côme-du-Mont, on Drop-Zone 'D'. (see Map opposite).

The 101st Airborne Division essentially had six main objectives. First, they were to clear and secure the western exits of the four causeways over the marshland and floods leading to Utah Beach. This would then facilitate the seaborne assault which, on landing, would need only to clear the beach defences around the eastern exits before they could advance inland.

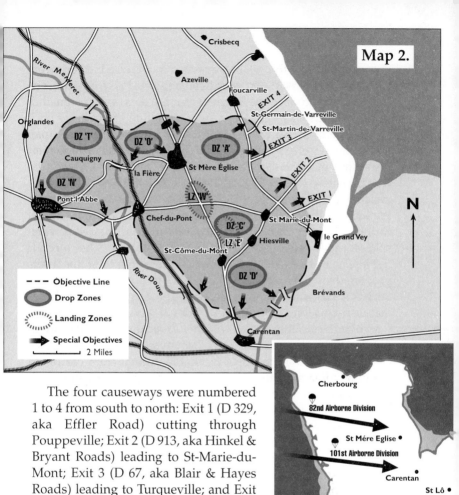

Map 2.

The four causeways were numbered 1 to 4 from south to north: Exit 1 (D 329, aka Effler Road) cutting through Pouppeville; Exit 2 (D 913, aka Hinkel & Bryant Roads) leading to St-Marie-du-Mont; Exit 3 (D 67, aka Blair & Hayes Roads) leading to Turqueville; and Exit 4 (D 423, aka Begel, Pritchett & Criss Roads cutting through St-Martin-de-Varreville).

The western exits of Beach Exits 1 and 2 were to be taken by the men of the 506th PIR that were to land at Drop Zone 'C', while to the north, Beach Exits 3 and 4 would be secured by the 502nd PIR.

The second objective, also given to the 502nd PIR, was to ensure that a German coastal battery, just west of St-Martin-de-Varreville, and a nearby barracks (identified as Position WXYZ) had been silenced by the Allied bombers. If the battery was still active though, then the airborne troops were to neutralise the area before pushing northwards and securing a third objective, defensive positions around Foucarville. This would then serve to block any German counter-attacks on the right flank of Utah

Beach. In addition, by establishing links with the 82nd Airborne Division to the West (around Beuzeville-au-Plain), the 502nd PIR would then form the link between the Airborne troops and the beachhead.

A fourth objective, for the 1/501st PIR, landing on Drop Zone 'D', was to capture the lock at la Barquette. The lock, which controlled the water level of the Rivers Douve and Merderet, was considered to be of vital strategic importance. If captured intact, the lock would give the Allies control of a natural barrier that could be used to help prevent the Germans from counterattacking the left flank of VII Corps during the early stages of the campaign.

However, the Germans, too, were aware that the lock could provide them with a natural barrier in this area of the Cotentin Peninsular against an airborne assault. Since November, 1942, the Germans had allowed the tide to flood the low lying marshland on either side of the River Douve and River Merderet. By closing the lock, when the tide receded, the Germans were able to prevent the marshlands from draining. Thus, by the end of the summer in 1943, when the floods had reached their maximum height, the Germans believed that they had established an effective deterrent to anyone considering airborne operations in this area.

Allied intelligence had indeed witnessed the floods as they had been taking aerial reconnaissance photographs of the region to monitor its progress. However, nature soon began to adjust to the changing environment and the tall grasses and reeds flourished in the flooded waters and provided a camouflage cover across the flooded areas. Allied intelligence then made a grave misjudgement. They assumed that the floods had receded and that the area had not been permanently flooded by the Germans.

As a result of that decision the Allied planners were no longer concerned with what dangers the marshland would pose to their airborne assault forces. Instead, they now concentrated their efforts on ways in which the lock and marshland could be used to their own advantage. Plans were then drawn-up to capture the locks intact so that the land could be flooded in the event of a German counter-offensive. It was a mistake that very nearly jeopardized the whole of the airborne operation and one which would cause chaos and cost the paratroopers dearly.

In April, 1944, maps were drawn up which correctly outlined the extent of the marshland. However, instead of a warning the maps were labelled with the misnomer *'ground here probably soft'*, an error that would not be fully realised until American airborne troops actually began landing in the deep waters and marshes around the Rivers Merderet and Douve.

The fifth objective of the 101st Airborne Division was for the 3/501st PIR, which would land at Drop Zone 'C'. Their task was to protect Landing Zone 'E', between St-Marie-du-Mont and le Forges (in the vicinity of DZ 'C') as it was in this area that the gliderborne reinforcements, for the 101st Airborne Division, were due to land at dawn in Operation 'Chicago'.

The Sixth and final objective for the 101st Airborne Division was for the 3/506th PIR, landing at DZ 'D', who were tasked with seizing two bridges across the River Douve, at le Port, and establishing a southern bridgehead which could later be exploited to form a link-up with the American troops of V Corps that had landed at 'Omaha' Beach.

82nd Airborne Division[4]

The appearance of the German 91st Luftlande (airlanding) Division, in May, 1944, posed a serious threat to operations of the 82nd Airborne division. It had been planned that the 82nd would land west of St-Sauveur-le-Vicomte and prevent German reinforcements from moving freely in the western half of the Cotentin Peninsular. With another German division in the vicinity it was decided that the 82nd, in Operation 'Boston', would be dropped further east, on either side of the River Merderet, where they would be nearer the 101st Airborne Division and more able to secure the western sector for the Utah Beach landings.

The 82nd Airborne Division would take off just ten minutes after the 101st Airborne division had departed. Two parachute regiments, the 507th and 508th PIR, were to land west of the River Merderet on Drop-Zones 'T' and 'N' respectively, while to the east of the river, the 505th PIR (with elements of the 456th Parachute Field Artillery Battalion and 307th Airborne Engineer Battalion) and Divisional Commander, Major-General Ridgeway, were to land on Drop Zone 'O'.

The 82nd Airborne Division had five main objectives on D-Day. First they were to take and hold the market town of St-

Mère-Église, then they were to advance and secure their second objective which was the area to the north between Neuville-au-Plain and Beuzeville-au-Plain (thereby establishing a link with the 101st Airborne Division). Their third objective was to secure and hold the two road bridges, to the west of St-Mère Église, over the River Merderet at Chef-du-Pont (D 67) and la Fière (D15). These tasks were assigned to the men of the 505th PIR, though assistance would be given by the 507th PIR with regards the capture of the bridges at la Fière and Chef-du-Pont.

St-Mère-Église was particularly important because it was a key communication centre for the Germans, as it was ideally situated straddling *Route 13* (replaced today by the N 13, which now by-passes St Mère Église), the main road from Paris to Cherbourg.

After securing the Bridge at la Fière the 507th PIR were to then move towards their fourth objective which was to establish a defensive line, to the west, between Gourbesville and la-Croix-Renouf. These deep bridgeheads, over the River Merderet, were also to be held and defended in the south on a line along the River Douve. This fifth objective was to be accomplished by the 508th PIR who were tasked with the destruction of the bridges over the River Douve at Pont l'Abbé and Beuzeville-la-Bastille. The 508th PIR would then extend their line north to meet up with the 507th PIR at la-Croix-Renouf.

With these missions accomplished, and with the landings successful on Utah Beach, the 82nd Airborne Division would then continue with a westward offensive towards St-Sauveur-le-Vicomte. Thereby pushing the Germans back and continuing the process of sealing off the Cotentin Peninsular and isolating the port of Cherbourg.

Airborne Reinforcements[5]

At approximately 04.30 hrs (H-2 hrs) reinforcements, for the 82nd Airborne Division, would arrive by Horsa glider during Operation 'Detroit.' Landing at LZ 'O' these reinforcements would include some 220 troops, Jeeps, two batteries of the 80th AAA/AT Battalion, men from the 82nd Signal Company and staff from Headquarters.

At approximately the same time as the 'All American' division was being reinforced, fifty-two Waco gliders would also land at LZ 'E.' These gliders, in Operation 'Chicago,' would be carrying reinforcements for the 101st Airborne Division. The 'Screaming Eagles' aboard would be from two batteries of the 81st AAA/AT Battalion, elements of the 101st engineer, signal and medical companies, and also more staff officers including the assistant divisional commander, Brigadier-General Don Pratt. In total some 155 troops, 25 jeeps, a midget bulldozer and 166-pounder anti-tank guns.

Cloth insignia of the Troop Carrier Command.

Due to a shortfall in the number of aircraft available, a number of 101st Airborne Division units would be brought in by ship and land on Utah Beach. Amongst these were the 327th Glider Infantry Regiment (including 1/401st GIR), 321st and 907th Glider Field Artillery Battalion, 326th Airborne Engineer Battalion and the remaining units of he 81st AAA/AT Battalion. For the 82nd Airborne Division the seaborne contingent comprised of the 325th Glider Infantry Regiment (including 2/401st GIR).

Further airborne reinforcements would also arrive, by glider, on the evening of D-Day at 21.30 hrs (H+15 hrs). This time additional troops from the 101st Airborne Division, and supplies, would be transported by Horsa glider during Operation 'KEOKUK'.

For the 82nd Airborne Division there would also be more reinforcements during the evening of D-Day. Codenamed Operation 'Elmira,' 176 Waco and Horsa gliders would land in two waves, one around sunset and the other after dark. The first wave would bring in the remaining battery of the 80th AAA/AT Battalion, and reconnaissance and headquarters staff, totalling some 437 men.

With them they would also bring sixty-four Jeeps and additional weapons and supplies to LZ 'W.' The second wave would bring in the 319th and 320th Glider Field Artillery Battalion.

Additional airborne reinforcements for the 82nd Airborne Division, which included part of the 325th Glider Infantry Regiment, would be brought in by air on D+1. Landing on LZ 'W,' in Waco and Horsa gliders, they would be transported to their LZ in Operation 'Galveston' and 'Hackensack.'

Aerial and Naval Support

One hour before the seaborne assault onto the beach at 'Utah', at 05.20 hrs, 276 B26 Marauder medium bombers[6] of the 9th U.S. Air Force would attack seven main German defence positions along Utah Beach.

The Western Task Force (TF 122) was the naval formation that would support, land and protect the U.S. First Army as they made their assault onto the beaches at Utah and 'Omaha.' Though the overall command of this force was with Rear-Admiral Alan G. Kirk,

Admirial Sir Birtram Ramsey (left) and Rear Admiral Alan Kirk.

command for the naval force assigned to Utah Beach, Task Force 125 (Force 'U'), was given to the 'overly cautious,' but industrious, Rear-Admiral Don P. Moon. For the invasion itself Rear-Admiral Moon would oversee the landing of the U.S. 4th and 90th Infantry Division (and supporting units) while anchored some thirteen miles off the Cotentin Peninsular in his flag ship the USS *Bayfield*.

As the US 9th Air Force dropped some 500 tons of bombs onto the German defences, the US naval Bombardment Group, under the command of Rear-Admiral Morton. L. Deyo, would provide additional covering fire: the battleship USS *Nevada*, with its 14 inch guns, would attempt to neutralize the German Battery at Azeville. Meanwhile, two American cruisers (USS *Tuscaloosa* and *Quincy*), three British cruisers (HMS *Hawkins*, *Enterprise* and *Black Prince*), a Dutch gunboat (*Soemba*), and a British Monitor (HMS *Erebus*) would direct their guns at other targets in the area. In addition a further eight destroyers and two escorts were also available in the bombardment group.[7]

Under this covering fire the assault force, in their LCVP's (Landing Craft Vehicle Personnel) and LCT's (Landing Craft Tank), would make their way towards the shoreline. In support, for the actual beach landing, some thirty-two Duplex Drive tanks* would also be heading for the shore ready to land along with the first waves.

When the first wave of landing craft were within 700 yards of

---

* Duplex Drive tanks were modified Sherman tanks that had a waterproofed underside and a collapsible canvas screen which surrounded the turret. Fitted with twin propellers the 'Duplex Drive' tank could be propelled through calm seas onto the shoreline. On reaching the beach the vehicle's drive would be switched to its tracks, the canvas screen dropped, and the tank could then move forward straight into battle.

the shore thirty-three LCG's (Landing Craft Gun) and LCR's (Landing Craft Rocket) would provide additional covering fire by drenching the beach with rockets and machine-gun fire. If successful, the aerial and naval bombardments would incapacitate the German defenders, or at very least daze and confuse them, to such an extent that the enemy defences could be overpowered quickly and the US 4th and 90th Infantry Division could quickly establish a bridgehead on Utah Beach.

The naval support for the Utah Beach landings, Task Force 125, was massive (as was the support for the other four beach landings). The force was divided into six groups for the landings: Force Flagship Group, Minesweeper Group, Assault Group, Escort Group, Bombardment Group and Far Shore Service Group. In total, some 865 vessels, from landing craft to battleships, were to be used in this sector for the seaborne landings. Aboard, some 30,000 men and 3,500 vehicles, most of whom were ready to be landed onto Utah Beach on D-Day.[8]

4th, 90th, 9th & 79th Infantry Division

The seaborne troops would begin disembarking from their landing craft onto Utah Beach at H-Hour, 06.30 hrs. However, two hours before, a detachment from the 4th and 24th Cavalry Squadron, 4th Cavalry Group, would land on the heavily mined Iles St. Marcouf to neutralise the German defences. These two small islands lay some four miles off-shore and were in a position adjacent to the area where the landing craft would be assembled before they launched their attack onto Utah Beach. The potential threat that these islands posed to the invasion fleet was too great to be ignored, therefore, a unit was selected to clear the islands of any enemy resistance at 04.30 hrs.

The task and objective of the US 4th Infantry Division, supported by elements of the 90th Infantry Division, were to land on the beach at Utah and overpower the German defenders along the coastline. This completed they were to establish contact and reinforce the American airborne divisions and then push west and north-west to seal off the Cotentin Peninsular and capture the coastal port of Cherbourg.

Further reinforcements would arrive on D+4, with the arrival of the 9th Infantry Division. Later still, on D+8, the 79th division would also begin landing, and be temporarily attached to VII Corps.[9]

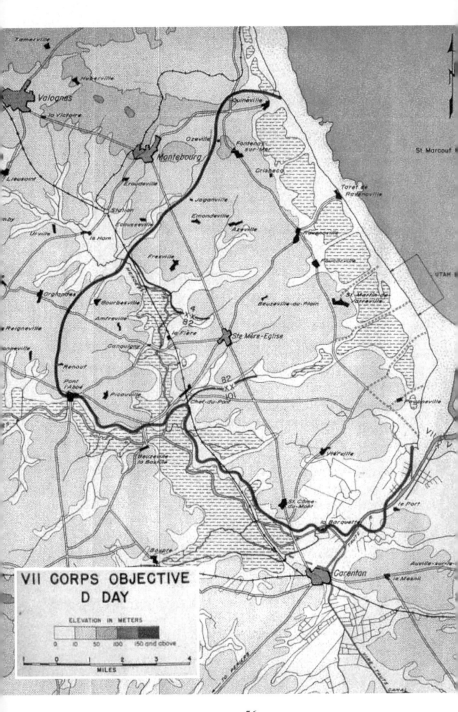

VII CORPS OBJECTIVE
D DAY

ELEVATION IN METERS

0   10   50   100   150 and above

0   1   2   3   4
MILES

The lessons learned during the raid on the French coastal town of Dieppe, back in August 1942, had made the COSSAC planners realise that it would be difficult for any major port to be captured quickly or intact. It was hoped, however, that Cherbourg would be captured by D+8 (though General Bradley did not think that this would be possible until D+15).[10]

Cloth insignia of the 9th Infantry Division.

Work could then begin on repairing the inevitable damage the Germans would inflict on the port facilities before surrendering, and Cherbourg could then be made good for supplies and reinforcements. The use of such a large port would greatly facilitate the build-up of troops and supplies needed to allow the Allies to break out of the Normandy bridgehead as quickly as possible. The build-up, in the meantime, would be made by landing supplies directly onto Utah Beach, a task that was to be organized and operated by the 1st Special Service Brigade. The 1st SSB would also ensure that all the necessary installations needed for the debarkation of troops

Cloth insignia of the 79th Infantry Division.

and supplies, and for evacuating the wounded and German Prisoners-of-War, were put in place and operating satisfactorily. A task that was in addition to their other operations, included the clearing of enemy beach obstacles, minefields, beach defences and securing the area around Utah Beach.

The initial assault onto Utah Beach would take place on the area codenamed 'Uncle Red' and 'Tare Green' (see Map 3 p104/105); with the 'Uncle Red' sector being positioned directly opposite 'Exit 3', one of the four causeways over the flooded marshland that could provide any access to and from the beach area.

The first troops ashore would be from the 8th Infantry Regiment, 4th Infantry Division, Aided by the 32 Duplex Drive tanks of the 70th Tank Battalion, 6th Armoured Group. Beach Obstacle Demolition Parties (BODP) of the 237th Engineer Combat Battalion (ECB), 1106th Engineer Combat Group, would also land in the first waves and begin their task of clearing the beach obstacles for the following troops and vehicles. To help them with their tasks there would also be tankdozer teams from the 70th Tank Battalion and 612th Light Equipment Company. Scattered amongst the combat troops would also be the medics who would then be on hand to tend the wounded during the assault.

The planners had previously decided that the Normandy landings would take place on a day when half-tide, on the Cotentin Peninsular, would be some forty minutes after dawn (thereby giving the air and naval forces some time to identify enemy land targets and make their bombardments more effective).

By landing on a flooding tide there would be the advantage that the landing craft, having landed their troops, could refloat with the aid of the incoming tide. In addition there would also be the advantage that the demolition teams, tasked with destroying or removing the beach obstacles, could carry out their tasks in dry conditions. Landing at half-tide was also important as this would allow the troops and vehicle to manoeuvre on the beach as they attacked the enemy strongpoints.

The final consideration, in selecting the H-Hour and D-Day, for the landings in Normandy was in choosing a time when conditions were favourable for the airborne units. For this the tidal requirements would have to be preceded by a night with a late rising full moon. The hours of darkness before the moon rose would help the invasion force remain hidden from any enemy observation while the full moon, when it appeared, would help illuminate the drop-zones for the paratroopers as they descended and assembled in Normandy. These predictable factors only coincided for three days in any month. The only factor that remained, which could not be predicted, was the weather conditions. That was a matter that could only be left to fate.

The German Defences

Hitler had appointed Generalfeldmarschall Karl Gerd von Rundstedt as *Oberbefehlshaber* West (OB West) back in March, 1942. Despite his title, von Rundstedt in fact had little authority. Hitler had issued his Directive Number 40, at the same time that von Rundstedt was appointed Commander-in-Chief in the West, which give von Rundstedt the responsibility of protecting the 1,700 miles of coastline from the Spanish border to Holland (plus another 300 miles of coastline on the Mediterranean).[11] However, because Hitler had issued an order that effectively divided and complicated the whole command hierarchy and system of power, it meant that no single commander, with the exception of the Führer himself, ever had total command of all the forces in this area. A matter that was noted by von Rundstedt's Chief of Staff, Generalleutnant Guenther Blumentritt:

Generalfeldmarschall **Erwin Rommel (left) and** *Generalfeldmarschall Gerd* **Von Rundstedt.**

> *The Commander-in Chief in the West (Rundstedt) was only the highest strategic and tactical authority, with the task of defending the coast against invasion. Only within this narrow framework could he give orders to the Luftwaffe and the Navy. Hence he was no Eisenhower, but a primus inter pares.*[12]

Generalleutnant **Guenther Blumentritt.**

After repeated appeals by von Rundstedt for reinforcements, Hitler eventually responded by appointing Generalfeldmarschall Erwin Rommel as Inspector General of the Atlantic Wall in November, 1943. Rommel, however, disagreed with von Rundstedt's anti-invasion plans, von Rundstedt believed that the coastline should be only lightly protected and that the bulk of his strategic forces should be further inland. Thus when the invasion occurred his infantry forces could manoeuvre and contain the area where the Allies had committed their invasion forces and his mobile armoured reserves could then be used to deliver a decisive counter-attack and throw the Allies back into the sea.

Rommel, in contradiction, favoured stopping the Allies on the

The 'Hedgehogs' which formed part of the beach defences.

shoreline. Aware of how the Allies had used their superior air-power in North Africa and Italy, Rommel was keenly aware that the Allies would use their air strength to prevent any reinforcements from being able to manoeuvre themselves towards the battlefield. If this occurred, and the majority of the German forces were effectively immobilized, then the Allied build-up would be unstoppable and total defeat certain.

In addition to the difference in tactics and strategy, Rommel and von Rundstedt also disagreed over where the actual

Generalfeldmarschall Rommel inspecting the beach defences in Normandy.

landings would take place; von Rundstedt believed that the invasion would take place across the Pas de Calais, while Rommel thought the Allies would favour an invasion in Normandy. Such differences in opinion, and the general weakness of the Atlantic Wall, prompted Rommel to advise Hitler that greater coastal defences were needed. Rommel also asked for, and received, command of the northern most divisions that controlled the most vulnerable areas of coastline, from the mouth of the River Loire in France, to the coastline along Belgium and Holland.

In January, 1944, von Rundstedt's command was divided into two Army Groups: Army Group B (comprising of 88 Corps in Holland, 15th Army from Antwerp to the River Orne, and 7th Army which covered the area from the River Orne to the River Loire) commanded by *Generalfeldmarschall* Rommel; and Army Group G (comprising of 1st Army along the Biscay coast and 19th Army in the South of France) commanded by General Blaskowitz.

On assuming his new command Rommel immediately began reinforcing and strengthening the Atlantic Wall. In orders issued to his field commanders Rommel made the urgency and importance of his instructions succinct and clear:

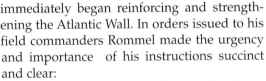

Mined 'Stake' beach defences.

In the short time left before the great offensive starts, we must succeed in bringing all defences to such a standard that they will hold up against the strongest attacks...The enemy must be annihilated before he reaches our main battlefield...We must stop him in the water, not only delaying him but destroying all his equipment while it is still afloat.'[13]

Generalfeldmarschall **Erwin Rommel, Commander, Army Group B.**

Within four months 500,000 beach obstacles and 4,000,000 land mines were laid along the coastline. Concrete pillboxes, fortified houses, coastal gun emplacements, artillery positions, machine gun posts, barbed wire fences and scores of other defensive positions were either reinforced or created

Generalfeldmarschall **Erwin Rommel.**

in order to ensure that any attack by the Allies could be met with substantial opposition. In order to deter any airborne landings Rommel had ordered that all open areas of land within seven miles of the coast were to be flooded, mined or have tall wooden post planted in them. Known as 'Rommel's Asparagus', some of these tall poles were also tipped with mines to act as an additional deterrent.

Rommel's battle plan was not without its critics though, in particular the commander of Panzer Group West, General Leo von Geyr von Schweppenburg. Like von Rundstedt, Geyr von Schweppenburg favoured holding the panzer divisions in reserve until they were confident that any Allied attack was a deliberate attempt to invade and establish a permanent bridgehead; as opposed to just a diversionary attack which would distract vital German reserves from another, and even greater, invasion elsewhere. Rommel however, was confident that everything must be thrown at the Allies within the first twenty-four hours.

At first he pleaded with von Rundstedt for control of the panzer divisions, when that failed, he then made an appeal direct to the Führer. Hitler, influenced by arguments on both sides made a compromise and gave Rommel control of only three of the Armoured Divisions; the 2nd, 21st and 116th Panzer Divisions. The three divisions were deployed thus: 21st Panzer Division near Caen, 2nd Panzer Division between the River Somme and the Pas de Calais, and 116th Panzer Division near Paris. However, the remaining Panzer Divisions, which remained under the command of von Rundstedt and Geyr von Schweppenburg as a strategic reserve, could not, in the increasingly complicated command structure, be committed to battle without the direct order of the Führer.[14]

The compromise suited neither Rommel or Geyr von Schweppenburg and the division of the panzer forces resulted in there being neither a strong tactical reserve of armour or a strong strategic reserve. Both commanders argued their case but Hitler's decision, or indecision, remained.

The German 7th Army
The area of the Cotentin Peninsular was defended by the German divisions of 84 Corps, commanded by General Erich Marcks which came under the command of the German 7th

Army and the tall, distinguished looking, *Generaloberst* Friedrich Dollmann (for full Order of Battle see Appendix B). Dollman had commanded the 7th Army since 1939 and, after breaking through the Maginot Line around Colmar in June, 1940, he had been assigned the occupation and defence of Normandy and Brittany.

By May 1944 the Germans had three full divisions (and elements of a fourth) on the Cotentin Peninsular. The 709th Infantry Division manned the coastal defences along Utah Beach up to Cherbourg and were tasked with preventing the Allies from landing on the beaches. The 243rd Infantry Division, defending the area on the west coast of the Cotentin Peninsular, had about half of its strength farther inland occupying an area of high ground with the orders to attack any airborne troops that landed.

The recent addition of the 91st Luftlande Division, which had caused Allied commanders to alter the battle plan for the 82nd Airborne Division, occupied the central area of the Cotentin Peninsular astride the River Merderet and around Carentan and Lessay. To the southeast, elements of the 352nd Infantry Division, which formed part of the defences on 'Omaha' Beach, occupied the area around Isigny.

Unknown to Allied Intelligence, Rommel had asked Hitler in May 1944, to move one of their reserve panzer divisions farther east. Rommel had suggested that the 12th SS (Hitler Jugend) Panzer Division be moved to the area around Carentan and St

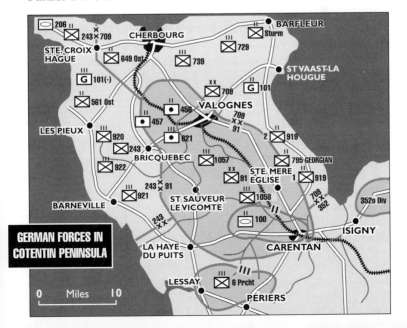

Lô, however, von Rundstedt had opposed the move. In the event, Hitler agreed with von Rundstedt and the 12th SS Panzer Division remained in the area between the River Seine and River Orne.[15]

German Air and Naval Power

Where the Germans knew they would be most vulnerable was in the air. On the 5th June, 1944, the German 3rd Air Force (*Luftflotten 3*), IX, X, and II Air Corps (*Fliegerkorps*), 2nd Fighter Corps (*Jagdkorps*) and Reconnaissance Group 122, reported a total fighting strength of 481 aircraft of which only 100 were fighters and sixty-four were reconnaissance planes. Because of disruption to the German communication systems, caused by Allied bombings and sabotage by SOE, SAS and the French Resistance movement, only 80 serviceable fighters of the 2nd and 26th Fighter Groups would be available in Normandy during the first two days of the invasion.[16] The Allies, by comparison, had 2,434 fighters and fighter-bombers operationally available plus an additional 700 light and medium bombers.[17]

The German Navy was another potential threat for the Allies as the convoys made their way towards the Normandy coastline. It was estimated that within the first few days of the invasion the Germans would have at their disposal some 130 U-boats, 5 destroyers, 9-11 torpedo boats, 50-60 E-boats, 50-60 R-boats, 25-30 'M' class mine sweepers and 60 miscellaneous craft.[18]

Therefore, constant patrolling by RAF Coastal Command and the Royal Navy was necessary to ensure that no German vessels could reach the vast invasion fleet and disrupt their transportation of troops onto the Normandy coastline.

The Final Decision

While the weather in the first week of June caused the Allied Commanders great concern, it gave the Germans a false sense of security. On 4 June Major Lettue, the chief meteorologist with the 3rd Air Force, issued a weather forecast that indicated that the Allies would be unable to invade in the next fourteen days.[19] This prompted Rommel to leave Normandy and combine a visit to his wife, whose birthday was on the 6th June, with a visit to the Führer in order to make yet another plea for the remaining

General Dwight D. Eisenhower visits men of the 502nd PIR, 101st A/B Div. at Greenham Common on 5th June, 1944.

Panzer reserve to be put under his command and deployed where he saw fit.

The inclement weather also served to ground most of Germany's reconnaissance planes and keep its naval patrol boats in harbour. Therefore, on the 4 June, 1944, under the protection of the storm that threatened to completely disrupt their operations, the Allied naval forces destined for American beaches of Utah and 'Omaha', which had farthest to travel, were put to sea. As the heavy seas tossed and battered their ships the men aboard awaited the news that would set them on course for the Normandy beaches.

Group Captain Stagg, SHAEF's chief meteorologist, had reported to Eisenhower at 4.00am on the morning of the 4th June that the weather outlook was unfavourable. Eisenhower postponed the operation for twenty-four hours and awaited the next weather report which would be made at 9.00pm that evening. The evening forecast proved to be more optimistic and the provisional order was given that the invasion would take place on the 6 June. The final, and irrevocable, order was given seven hours later at 4.15 am on Monday 5 June.

That evening General Dwight D. Eisenhower decided that he

would visit some of the troops that would be participating in the initial assault.

> *A late evening visit on the 5th took me to the camp of the U.S. 101st Airborne Division, one of the units whose participation had been so severely questioned by the air commander. I found the men in fine fettle, many of them joshingly admonishing me that I had no cause for worry, since the 101st was on the job and everything would be taken care of in fine shape. I stayed until the last of them were in the air, somewhere about midnight. After a two-hour trip back to my own camp, I had only a short time to wait until the first news should come in.*[20]
>
> **General Dwight D. Eisenhower, Supreme Commander of the Allied Expeditionary Force.**

The next twenty-four to forty-eight hours would now be amongst the hardest, and longest, of Eisenhower's career. For in that time he would learn whether he had indeed made the right-decision. Operation 'Overlord' would soon enter the history books as either the most remarkable invasion in history or the greatest military blunder of all time. Whatever the outcome though one thing was for sure, that night there would begin a bloodletting that would not be stopped until one side or the other was completely destroyed. The Battle for Normandy was about to begin.

1. op. cit. Crookenden, Napier. p.34.
2. Andrews, John. *Airborne Album, Normandy.* (Phillips Publications, Inc., Williamstown, 1994). p.8.
3. op. cit. *Utah Beach to Cherbourg Report.*
4. ibid.
5. op. cit. Andrews, John. pp.39, 40, 46, 47& 48.
6. op.cit. *Utah Beach to Cherbourg Report.* p.43.
7. Chandler, David G. (editor) *The D-Day Encyclopedia.* (Simon & Schuster, New York, 1994). p.593.
8. Wilmot, Chester. *The Struggle for Europe.* (Reprint Society Ltd., London, 1954). P.270.
9. Revised Field Orders issued 28 May, 1944.
10. op. cit. Wilmot, Chester. p.230.
11. ibid. pp.200-201.
12. Blumentritt, Guenther von Rundstedt. *The Soldier and the Man* (Odhams Press Ltd., London, 1952). p.125.
13. Letter of Instructions, for Army Commanders, dated 22 April, 1944.
14. op. cit. Wilmot, Chester. p.307.
15. ibid.
16. Galland, Adolf. *The First and the Last.* (Transworld Publishers Ltd., London, 1958). pp.331-332
17. op. cit. *The Eisenhower Report.* p.14.
18. ibid. p.23.
19. op. cit. Wilmot, Chester. p.245.
20. op. cit. Eisenhower, Dwight D. p.277.

CHAPTER FOUR

THE AIRBORNE ASSAULT

Take Off

Late on the evening of the 5 June, 1944, the 502nd PIR, 377th Parachute Field Artillery Battalion, and 326th Airborne Medical Company, of the 101st Airborne Division, began their departure from Greenham Common. From Welford, witnessed by the Supreme Commander, General Dwight D. Eisenhower, the C-47 Dakotas of the 435th Troop Carrier Group, carrying the HQ staff and 3/501st PIR, climbed into the night sky and circled until all the aircraft had taken-off and joined the formation.

At seven other airfields across England the scene was the

An American Paratrooper from 506th PIR 101st A/B Div. climbs aboard a Dakota C-47 transport plane.

Captain Frank Lillyman's Pathfinder Team Stick No1, the first American troops into Normandy on D-Day.

same. American paratroopers of the 101st Airborne Division, weighted so heavily with their equipment that they could hardly walk, were squeezed into their aircraft sixteen or eighteen to a stick. As soon as all the aircraft had joined formation the vast armada of 432 Dakotas[1] began their journey heading for the Cotentin Peninsular and towards their rendezvous with destiny.

Thirty minutes prior to the 101st Airborne Division's take-off 20 Pathfinder teams, with some 300 Pathfinder paratroopers, departed from North Witham, near Grantham, in Lincolnshire.

Pathfinder Stick No.6 501st PIR 101st A/B Div.

Ten minutes after the 101st Airborne Division was airborne, the 82nd Airborne Division began their take-off in another 369[2] Dakotas, from five airfields in Lincolnshire. However, a serious accident at one of the airfields, Spanhoe, prevented one of the planes from taking off. While the paratroopers were settling down in their aircraft a grenade accidentally exploded in the aircraft fuselage. The plane was wrecked and three men were killed instantly (a fourth died later, in the early hours of the 6th June, from his wounds). Two of the four killed, Corporal Kenneth A.Vaught and Private First Class Robert L. Leakey, are buried in the Cambridge American Cemetery and Memorial (see Appendix C).

The two other troopers killed, Private Eddie Meelberg, who died of his wounds and Private Pete Vah, were flown back home to the United States at the request of their families.

In addition, all but one of the stick were wounded by the flying shrapnel. The unscathed survivor, Corporal Melvin Fryer,[3] was unperturbed though and subsequently managed to find a place aboard another Dakota.

During the initial phase of the Normandy landings, Operation Neptune, the USAAF IX Troop Carrier Command dispatched 1,662 aircraft and 512 gliders. In total some 17,262 troops, 110 Jeeps, 504 artillery weapons and over 2,000,000, lbs of combat equipment and supplies were dropped, behind enemy lines, into Normandy.[4]

The weather in and around the drop zones that night and following morning was cloudy, with a westerly wind blowing at fifteen knots. The cloud ceiling was at 10,000 ft but there were also clouds at 1000 ft.[5] In addition low-lying mist and fog obscured some of the landmarks and checkpoints for the pilots and paratroopers.

As the pilots flew their aircraft across the Cotentin Peninsular, from west to east, they began to encounter heavy ack-ack fire from the German anti-aircraft guns, nevertheless the first stick of Pathfinders was dropped into Normandy at 00.16hrs, 6 June, 1944. They would be followed, approximately one hour, later by the main drop of the 101st and then the 82nd Airborne Division.

The first American troops into Normandy on D-Day* were

* The question of who were the first Allied troops to land in Normandy, on D-Day, has been a constant source of controversy and discussion between the British and Americans for many years. The information gathered by this author, however, indicates that Captain Frank Lillyman and his Pathfinder team, from the US 101st Airborne Division, landed at 00.16 hrs; the same time as Major John Howard and his assault troops, from the British 6th Airborne Division, landed at Pegasus Bridge.

Troops from the 325th Glider Infantry Regiment 82nd A/B Div. aboard a Horsa Glider.

Captain Frank Lillyman's Pathfinder Team from the 502nd PIR, 101st Airborne Division, which landed about a mile away from DZ 'A.' Other Pathfinder drops were also scattered and disrupted during the airborne assault; an indication of the trouble that lay ahead.

One of the Dakotas carrying the Pathfinders had lost an engine while crossing the English Channel and began a return journey, with the Pathfinders still aboard, until it was forced to ditch in the sea. Fortunately all the troops and crew were rescued by a nearby destroyer.

The remaining Pathfinder teams all dropped on time but only a few landed on their designated drop or landing zone. In addition, as a result of the confusion and tension created by the weather and German flak, many were dropped at too high, or too low, an altitude. In addition some of the pilots were flying over the area too fast, which created an added danger for the Pathfinders and resulted in the loss and damage of some of their equipment.

Only a few of the Pathfinders, landing at DZ 'O' and DZ 'T,' were successfully dropped on their target and managed to set up some of their equipment in the right place. The rest were dispersed over a much wider area which meant that some of the navigational equipment was in the wrong area (up to a mile away from where is should have been). The confusion caused by the scattered drops was then further complicated as a result of some Pathfinders being dropped near or amongst German troop positions. The ensuing fire-fights resulting in some of the Pathfinders not deploying their equipment at all. Subsequently the Pathfinders suffered the first American combat casualties during the Normandy Campaign.

Discovering the identity of the first fatal casualties was a task undertaken in the 1960s by the 101st Airborne Division's historian, George E. Koskimaki, and Captain Frank Lillyman, commanding officer of the Pathfinder Teams.

The evidence of their research indicates that the men of Second-Lieutenant Charles Faith's Pathfinder Team, 501st PIR, who were heading for DZ 'C' were the first to be engaged by the enemy when they hit the ground.

As the 6th Pathfinder stick to jump into Normandy they exited their aircraft at 00.25 hrs. According to the reports that were assessed Private J. McDougall drowned on landing and Private Stanley Suwarsky was caught up in a tree and was killed by machine-gun fire before he could free himself. Private Suwarsky was later buried in the Normandy American Military Cemetery and Memorial (see appendix C), while Private McDougall's body was repatriated to the United States.

This first drop, involving just twenty aircraft, was to be a predictor of events to come. The Pathfinder drops could, quite accurately, be described as a confused and disrupted affair; for what followed, involving over 800 aircraft and 13,000[7] paratroopers, the only suitable word would be 'chaos'.

The Main Airborne Assault
As the aircraft carrying the 'Screaming Eagles' approached the Normandy coastline they were faced with the scattered cloud and fog that had affected the Pathfinders. The strict

American airborne troops at their most vulnerable.

formation of the transports still held though up to the point that the German anti-aircraft and tracer fire began peppering the air around the C-47s.

Some of the pilots had never flown in combat before and were disturbed by the seemingly impenetrable wall of flak that faced them. So the aircraft formation began to break-up as some pilots began taking evasive action or were disorientated by the noise and bright flashes of the tracer and anti-aircraft fire. The jinking of the aircraft by the pilots didn't help the paratroopers prepare for their jump, additionally it also made it harder for the navigators to locate the drop zone. The combination of the Pathfinder problems, weather, German fire and aircrew reactions, resulted in the 101st Airborne division being dropped all over the Cotentin Peninsular. While a few sticks were actually dropped onto their designated drop zone, some sticks came to ground up to twenty-one miles from their DZ.

The 82nd Airborne Division fared little better either, with some sticks being dropped between thirteen and twenty-five miles from their DZ. Of over 300 sticks dropped into Normandy only fifty-one were successfully dropped onto their drop zone.[8]

The greatest problem that faced the two airborne divisions, after the parachute drops, was how to group all the men into organized and collective fighting units capable of carrying out all the tasks that had been assigned to them. One result of such scattered drops, and the consequence it can have on the enemy, has been described, by an anonymous writer on airborne operations, as the rule of LGOP's (Little Groups of Paratroopers):

After the demise of the best Airborne plan, a most terrifying effect occurs on the battlefield. This effect is known as the rule of LGOP's. This is, in its purest form, small groups of pissed-off 19-year old paratroopers...[who are] well-trained, armed to the teeth and lack serious adult supervision. They collectively remember the Commander's intent as 'March to the sound of the guns and kill anyone who is not dressed like you...' or something like that.

Despite the obvious problems having so many paratroopers wandering around without a leader, would have on the operational objectives of the airborne assault, the displacement of so many troops would also have a positive effect. Troops, dispersed over an area of more than 250 square miles, brought about conflicting reports of enemy attacks to the headquarters of the local German garrisons. The sporadic fighting all over the peninsular made it difficult, at the time, for any of the German commanders to ascertain the planned objectives of such an assault. It was not long before word of the Allied airborne assault had reached the German Commander-in-Chief West, Generalfeldmarschall von Rundstedt.

> *On 6 June, between two and three o'clock in the morning, General* [-leutnant] *Speidel* [Rommel's Chief-of-Staff] *reported personally that parachute jumps and air landings by glider had taken place on the Cotentin Peninsular. The tactical time of these landings from the air was 00.30 to 01.30 hours, that is, shortly after midnight. New inward flight were continuously reported in Normandy. Night fighting had already broken out with the enemy who had landed, but details were not yet known.*
> Generalleutnant **Guenther Blumentritt, CoS, OB West.**

While the report of glider landings at this time was incorrect the rest was most certainly true. Immediately the German commanders set about trying to determine whether these landings were the real invasion or just a diversionary attack to

Captain Frank Lillyman of the Pathfinders at Foucarville on 6th June 1944, the first American soldier to land in Normandy on D-Day.

draw the Germans' attention and manpower away from another more decisive assault. *Generalfeldmarschall* von Rundstedt was soon convinced that the attack on the Cotentin Peninsular was indeed part of the real invasion; why else, he reasoned, would the Allies expend so many valuable airborne troops in an assault.

What remained though was to convince the Armed Forces High Command, and more importantly the Commander-in-Chief of the Army, Adolf Hitler, that measures should be taken straight away to repel these attacks. As news filtered through of airborne attacks east of the River Orne, efforts were then made, by the Commander-in-Chief West, to try and order two of Hitler's strategic reserves, to an area in the direction of Caen and St Lô.[9]

12th SS Panzer Division move as quickly as possible in direction of Lisieux. Panzer Instructional [Lehr] *Division form up ready to move off at Alert station. Both divisions on entering the field of operations will be under orders of Army Group B.*
Generalfeldmarschall von Rundstedt, OB West.

These orders were, however, countermanded by the Wehrmacht Headquarters who berated Western Command for trying to issue orders without the Führer's approval. The result was that the two panzer divisions were stopped from making their way towards the invasion area. Hitler did release the two panzer divisions to Army Group West later that day, but by then it was too late for the units to have any effect on D-Day.

The confusion created by the airborne assault, in conjunction with Operation 'Fortitude' (the deception plans of SHAEF), left the German High Command unsure of what was happening. This indecision on the part of the German commanders helped give the airborne forces a much needed breathing space to establish themselves.

The scattered parachute drops of the airborne divisions resulted in many commanding officers being forced to accommodate and assign men of other units, into their battalions. Only this way could the officers have any chance of building their numbers into a sizable fighting force so that they could continue with orders and tasks that had been assigned to them.

St Mère Église

St Mère Église is just off the **N13**, the main road from **Caen/Bayeux** to **Cherbourg**. Following the road signs directing you to the town drive into the town square (called Place du 6 June) along Rue du D.D. Eisenhower and park your car in the car park adjacent to the church. Walk across to the south-east side of the square, opposite the church entrance, and stand next to the green railings facing the church. Look closely at the railings to see evidence of the fighting that took place here. On the church tower (during the summer months) you will see a mannequin of a paratrooper hanging from a stone buttress which represents Private John

Evidence of bullet marks in St Mère Église today.

Steele. To your right, along the tree-lined road which leads down the side of the church, there is an old hand-powered water pump which was used by the villagers to extract water to help put out a house fire back in 1944, the house where the Airborne Museum is now located.

The 82nd Airborne Division's Commanding officer, Major-General Matthew B. Ridgeway, and his head-quarters staff were to land alongside

Water pump used by villagers on the night 5/6th June, 1944 to put out a house fire.

the men of the 505th PIR, and elements of the 456th PFAB, on Drop Zone 'O'. The 505th PIR were tasked with taking St Mère Église and the area to the north, around Neuville-au-Plain, and east, at la Fière Bridge over the River Merderet.

Though the 505th experienced the most successful drop of all the parachute regiments, with thirty-one of the 118 sticks landing on the drop-zone, others were dropped up to fourteen miles away.[10]

Amongst those descending outside their drop zone area were some of the men of a mortar platoon, 'F' Company, 3/505th PIR, and some

St Mère Eglise Church with the mannequin of Private John Steele.

men of the 2/505th PIR, who found themselves heading towards the town square in the centre of St Mère Église.

On this night the local villagers had been allowed to break curfew in order to help put out a house fire next to the square.

The church bells tolled, announcing to the villagers that help was needed in the square. Under the watchful gaze of the German troops from the local garrison, the villagers formed a human chain at a nearby water pump and began passing buckets of water along towards the firemen that were tackling the raging fire.

At the same time wave upon wave of Dakotas were flying overhead and began dropping their loads of paratroopers. As the men of F Company began dropping in the square the German sentries instantly opened fire. Instinctively the villagers began running for cover. As the stick of paratroopers landed in the town square the Germans began shooting them before they could release themselves from their parachute harness. As Private John Steele came down to earth, the air was thick with flak and tracer fire from which he received a wound to his foot. Unable to control his decent he found himself swinging in his parachute harness and heading directly for the church steeple. There, on the central tower of the church, his parachute snagged on a stone pinnacle and Private John Steele found himself hanging, unable to move, from the church tower. Beneath him the Germans continued to slaughter the paratroopers that were landing all around them. A second paratrooper, Private Ken Russel, also landed on the church but slid down the roof before his parachute lines became snagged.

Almost immediately a Nazi soldier came running from the back side of the church shooting at everything. Sergeant John Ray had landed in the church yard, almost directly below Steele. The Nazi shot him in the stomach while he was still in his chute.[11]   **Private Ken Russel, F Company, 3/505th PIR, 82nd A/B Div.**

Before the German was able to cast his attention to Private Russel, the Sergeant, despite his mortal wound, managed to draw his pistol from its holster and shoot the German in the back of the head.

Retrieving his fighting knife Private Russel wasted no time and sliced his way through his parachute lines and fell, uninjured, to the ground. Quickly freeing and loading his rifle the trooper then made off away from the open square to the relatively safe shadows of the nearby streets and buildings trying to find more of his comrades.

Others were less fortunate. Private First Class Alfred J. van Holsbeck's descent carried him towards the roaring flames of the burning building. The heat of the fire appeared to draw the parachute towards it and the paratrooper descended into the inferno. Another trooper, Sergeant Edward White, also met with the same fate. The ammunition they were carrying served to fuel the flames and made the fire burn even more intensely.

During this time other paratroopers became snagged on power line poles or in tree branches as they descended. Amongst those killed while still in their parachute harness were Second-Lieutenant Harold Cadish, Private Charles Blankenship and Private Ladislaw Tlapa; Private H. T. Bryant Jr was also killed in the town square.

Private John Steele was desperate not to meet a similar fate as he watched the horrors below him. Suspended in his parachute harness he was unable free himself and so decided to feign death by hanging motionless, hoping that no Germans would

St Mère Eglise, 6th June, 1944 and a comparision shot today.

bother to waste any bullets on his seemingly lifeless body. During the carnage in the square a machine gun mounted in the belfry of the church fired down towards the ground.[12]

Also in the belfry were two German sentries on look-out, who were watching the paratroopers descending from the night sky.

Through an opening I saw a parachutist had fallen on the steeple, hanging by the ropes. He appeared to be dead, but after a moment I heard his voice. There were two of us at the post, and my companion wanted to shoot him.[13]

Obergefreiter Rudolph May, 919th Grenadier Regiment, 709th Infantry Division

Private John Steele was not shot however, and instead the German sentries freed him from his parachute and made him a prisoner-of-war.

Elsewhere, in the meantime, the 82nd Airborne Division were beginning to organize themselves into fighting units. Within a couple of hours Lieutenant-Colonel Edward Krause, 3/505 PIR, had gathered 180 men and had advanced towards St Mère Église. Splitting his force up into six sections, one to block each of the five roads into the town and another to clear the centre of St Mère Église, Lt-Col Krause then made his way into the centre of the town, guided by a local Frenchman who had offered to help.

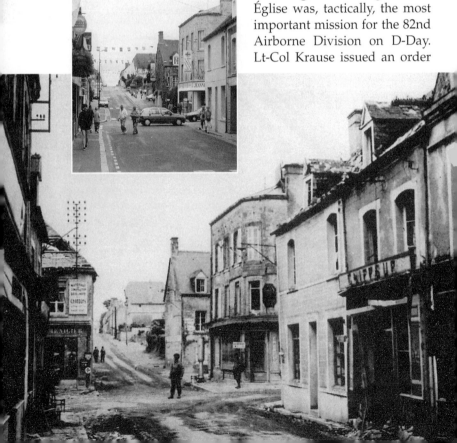

Taking and holding St Mère Église was, tactically, the most important mission for the 82nd Airborne Division on D-Day. Lt-Col Krause issued an order

to his men that no firearms were to be used, until daylight, during their attack in the town. Grenades, knives and bayonets were the only weapons to be used during the fight.[14]

Any small arms fire therefore was to be considered hostile and dealt with accordingly. At 04.30hrs[15] Lt-Col Krause raised the Stars and Stripes above the town hall at St Mère Église (the same flag that the regiment had raised in the city of Naples in Italy back in October 1943). By 06.00 hrs the town had been secured, the Americans having killed forty-one of the German troops and taken another thirty prisoner.[16]

Lt-Col Krause, Commander of 3/505.

Lt-Col Krause had sent two messages to Colonel William E. Ekman, commanding officer of the 505th PIR, in the past two hours. The first confirming that he had entered the town, the second confirming its capture, however, for some unknown reason neither message reached the Colonel, though the second message did reach the Divisional Commander Maj-Gen Ridgeway.

Unaware of Lt-Col Krause's success and concerned over what was happening in St Mère Église, Colonel Ekman ordered Lieutenant-Colonel Benjamin H. Vandervoort, who was to secure the northern village of Neuville-au-Plain and the area to the east around Baudienville with his 2/505th PIR, to stop his advance. Two hours later a further order was received ordering his battalion to attack St Mère Église.

Lt-Col Vandervoort had been injured during his landing sustaining a fractured ankle and at the time he received his new orders he was being transported around in a small ammunition cart that had been appropriated for his use. Some 575 men of the 2nd Battalion had assembled out of the 630 that had jumped.[17]

So, despite the orders to take St Mère Église, Lt-Col

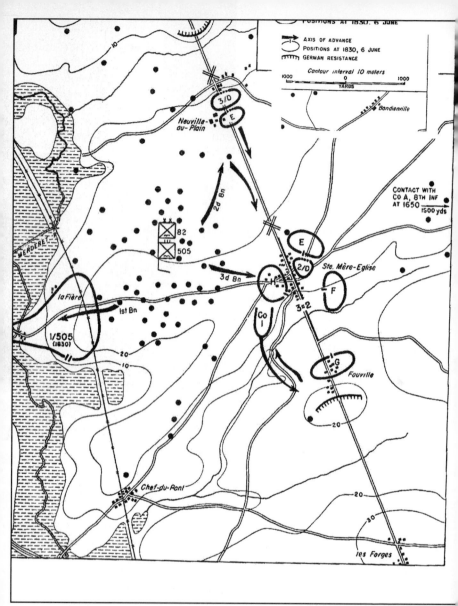

AXIS OF ADVANCE
POSITIONS AT 1830, 6 JUNE
GERMAN RESISTANCE

Contour interval 10 meters

1000   0   1000
YARDS

Bandienville

Neuville-au-Plain

2d Bn

CONTACT WITH
CO A, 8TH INF
AT 1650 — 1500 yds

82
505

E

2/0

Ste. Mère-Eglise

3d Bn

F

la Fière

1st Bn

Co
I

3=2

1/505
(1830)

G

Fouville

MERDERET

Chef-du-Pont

les Forges

Vandervoort decided also to continue with his original
objective. He then sent a platoon, led by Lieutenant Turner
Turnbull with forty-one men, towards Neuville-au-Plain with
orders to clear the village and set up a road-block. This platoon
found the village already clear of Germans and so were able to
establish their defences without any initial interference from the
Germans.

82

In the meantime Lt-Col Vandervoort had made his way into St Mère Église and soon became aware that the town had already been secured by Lt-Col Krause. After a discussion the two commanders decided that Lt-Col Vandervoort's 2nd Battalion would take over the defence positions in the northern part of the town thereby giving Lt-Col Krause more men to defend the rest of St Mère Église.

The extra men were soon to be needed. By 09.00 hrs German troops from the 795th Georgian Battalion had counter attacked from Hill 20, at Fauville, south-east of St Mère Église.

Supported by three tanks, two self-propelled guns and mortars, the Germans attempted to crush the 3rd Battalion's defences by putting their attack down either side of the road leading from Fauville to St Mère Église (Route 13). However, the American defences held and the Germans withdrew back to Hill 20. A counter-attack on Hill 20 by 'I' company of the 3/505th PIR proved unsuccessful and so a stalemate remained for the time being around the southern side of St Mère Église.

Lt-Col Benjamin H. Vandervoort on a crutch to help support his fractured ankle.

To the north, Lt-Col Vandervoort had taken a ride in a Jeep to see how Lieutenant Turnbull and his men were doing at Neuville-au-Plain. In addition his jeep was also towing a 6-pounder anti-tank gun, which had been brought in by glider only a few hours earlier, to help strengthen Lieutenant Turnbull's positions.

At around the same time that Turnbull arrived at Neuville-au-Plain, a German patrol was seen coming down the road towards them. In advance of the column was a Frenchman, riding a bicycle, who assured the Americans that the Germans were prisoners being escorted by American troops. However, Lt-Col Vandervoort suspected a ruse when Lieutenant Turner Turnbull's men saw German troops leaving the column and moving along the fields. The Frenchman had also quickly disappeared so Lieutenant Turner Turnbull's men were ordered

Aerial reconnissance photo.

to open fire. The fight at the road-block continued throughout the rest of the morning until by mid afternoon the Germans had nearly managed to surround the American paratroopers. With nearly half of his men killed or wounded Lieutenant Turnbull gave the order to withdraw to St Mère Église.

At St Mère Église the Germans were held back by the stronger forces. But the sacrifice of Lieutenant Turnbull's men had not been in vain, in holding the position at Neuville-au-Plain they had successfully protected the northern flank of the area where much of the 101st Airborne Division had landed. Unfortunately Lieutenant Turnbull was killed the following morning during a mortar attack.

La Fière Causeway

Drive from the square in St Mère Église back down Rue du Général D.D. Eisenhower to the western side of the town square. Turn right along the Rue Général de Gaulle and drive along to the

Brig-Gen Gavin's Foxhole. In the distance is La Fière Bridge.

second crossroad junction. Turn left onto the Rue de Verdun. Pass under the roadbridge **(N13)** and take the right fork in the road **(D15)** signposted Pont l'Abbe. Drive across the bridge over the railway line and then down the hill towards la Fière. As you descend down towards la Fière Bridge note on the left a chained off slit trench which is reputed to be, and posted as **2a** (see Appendix D), Brigadier General Gavin's Foxhole. Just before the bridge over the River Merderet, turn right after the sign post marked Memorial des Parachutistes, into the car park. On the high ground you will see the **2b**, Bronze Statue of 'Iron Mike'. Along the pathway leading to the statue are **2c**, 'A' Company, 505th PIR and the 80th AAA/AT Battalion, 82nd Airborne Division, Bronze Plaques. The 'Iron Mike' statue is dedicated to all the American airborne forces that landed on D-Day.

As you walk back to la Fière Bridge, in front of you is Manoir de la Fière and its farm buildings. To your right is la Fière Bridge which leads onto the causeway and along to Cauquigny.

The final objective for 1/505 PIR which, along with the help of 507th PIR, was to secure the western flank of St Mère Église by taking and holding the bridges over the River Merderet at la Fière and Chef-du-Pont.

Lieutenant John Dolan, commanding officer of 'A' Company, 1/505 and his men had a very successful drop having both landed only a 1,000 yards from their objective and managing to rally all but two of his 136 men within an hour of their drop. Tasked with taking the causeway and bridge and farm buildings (Manoir de la Fière) at la Fière, the men of 'A' Company approached the area but came under heavy machine-gun fire from the farm buildings, which stopped their advance.

Brigadier-General James M. Gavin, the assistant divisional commander, was in command of Force 'A' (which included the three parachute infantry regiments of the 82 A/B Div) and was responsible for securing the bridges across the River Merderet so that these could be exploited quickly by the rest of VII Corps. Having landed in an apple orchard west of the flooded River, Brig-Gen Gavin had assumed, initially, that he had landed farther south next to the River Douve. However, after a while when more men had gathered, including stragglers from the 508 PIR, Brig-Gen Gavin was able to recognise a railway embankment on the western side of the floods. Combined with the heavy gunfire he could hear coming from the east he correctly assumed that he had landed north of la Fière.

Brig-Gen Gavin set off for la Fière and met with Major Kellam, commanding officer of 1/505. Despite having only the one company ('A' Company), which was now making its way towards the farm buildings from a north-easterly direction, under the command of Lieutenant Dolan, Major Kellam assured Brig-Gen Gavin that the bridge and causeway would be taken and secured within the hour.

On hearing this the assistant divisional commander decided to move on to Chef-du-Pont and Hill 30 to find out what was happening there. After Brig-Gen Gavin's departure several attempts were made by Lieutenant Dolan's men to take the farm. However, the German defenders fought tenaciously and would give no ground.

> When we had travelled about two-thirds of the way up the hedgerow, they opened up on us with rifle, and at least two machine pistols. I returned fire with my Thompson Sub-Machine Gun at a point where I could see leaves in the hedgerow fluttering... As luck would have it, there was a German foxhole to my left which I jumped into and from where I continued to fire. I could only guess where to shoot, but I had to as part of the third platoon was exposed to their fire... The platoon was now under fire from two directions, from the point where I was pinned down, and also from the direction of the bridge.
>
> Lieutenant John D. Dolan, 'A' Company, 505 PIR, 82nd Airborne Division.

By mid morning Lieutenant Dolan's company strength was down nearly a third with twenty-one men wounded and ten dead.[18] The battle was proving to be more difficult than expected.

The fighting around le Fière was further complicated by the lack of communication equipment, and the scattered drop of the

507th PIR who were supposed to land on DZ 'T' and secure the western approaches leading to la Fière and the River Merderet.

So widely dispersed were the 507th PIR that only three[19] sticks managed to hit their drop zone. The majority of men landed in the flooded marshland on either side of the River Merderet.

The deep waters caught the airborne troops completely by surprise, they had only been expecting soft ground as detailed on the operation maps with which they had been briefed. Instead hundreds of paratroopers found themselves floundering in several feet of water. Fully laden with between sixty and ninety pounds of combat equipment many were unable to struggle free from their parachute harness and they were dragged down beneath the murky depths of the river. Some were more fortunate and were able to get out of their parachutes, but the cost of survival meant the loss of much of their equipment.

The 507th PIR, as a fighting unit, had been decimated by the drop. In the event it would be several days before enough stragglers were assembled to form a sizable force. In the

An unfortunate trooper of the 82nd A/B Div drowned in the flooded waters of the River Merderet.

meantime those that survived were trying to get their bearings; some had thought, incorrectly, that because they had landed in the water they must have landed farther south in the River Douve.

The railway embankment proved to be a lifeline for many of the troops that had survived their landing in the marshes. As time passed by more men assembled on the dry high ground of the embankment and began heading south towards la Fière. One such group of men made another attack on the farm buildings at la Fière led by Captain Ben Schwartzwalder, 507th PIR. This time the attack was made from the south side but heavy machine-gun fire stopped their advance.

Amongst those also in the marshes near la Fière were several sticks from the 508th PIR who were supposed to have been dropped on DZ 'N', including the regiment's commanding officer Colonel Leroy Lindquist. Colonel Lindquist had collected about 200 men within a couple of hours and like many others headed for the embankment. His intention was to move down to la Fière, cross the bridge, and then make for his objective Pont l'Abbe.

Brig-General Ridgeway.

On approaching la Fière from the east his group came under machine-gun fire from the farmhouse. At this stage, because all the radios had been damaged or lost, the three separate groups that had approached or attacked the farm buildings were unaware of each other's activities.

At about 11.00 hrs Brig-Gen Ridgeway arrived on the scene and met Colonel Lindquist. Hearing details of the situation from runners of the two other groups Maj-Gen Ridgeway ordered Colonel Lindquist to take command of all the troops in the vicinity. He was then to take the farm buildings and secure the bridge and causeway.

German infantrymen belonging to the 795th Georgian Battalion about two miles from St Mère Église.

At 12.00 hrs what was believed to be a coordinated attack began. Orders had been sent to Lieutenant Dolan's Company A to advance towards the farm buildings on the right flank, along the northern side near the road, while Captain Schwartzwalder's men attacked the left flank, to the south. Unfortunately the orders never reached Lieutenant Dolan so his company remained in their positions.

By midday one of Company A's patrols, led by Lieutenant Oakley, had eventually worked its way around the farm buildings, to the east and had reached the flooded river bank. Following orders issued to him earlier that morning by Lieutenant Dolan, Lieutenant Oakley's patrol had, by midday, positioned itself along the river bank and was ready to launch an attack. Amazingly, during the three hours of crawling through orchards and along hedgerows, the patrol had not encountered any of Captain Schwartzwalder's or Colonel Lindquist's men. What was even more amazing was that Lieutenant Oakley, by sheer coincidence, decided to launch his attack on the farm buildings just before noon when Captain Schwartzwalder was to put in his assault.

Lieutenant Oakley and Sergeant Oscar L. Queen made a dash for the cover of one of the farm walls under the covering fire of their men. The two paratroopers spotted and killed three

Germans including one that had begun to charge them firing his Schmeisser machine-gun pistol. Sergeant Queen ran across the farm driveway but was blown to the ground when a grenade exploded nearby. Shocked, but unhurt, he then heard a German sniper firing and spotted the culprit in the branches of a tree above where he lay. Sergeant Queen shot the sniper and also spotted a German machine-gun position. He then dashed back across the driveway to report what he had seen and a light machine-gun was brought up to the stone wall. A paratrooper then fired into the rear of the German machine-gun nest killing all the occupants.

As Lieutenant Oakley prepared to launch an all-out attack on the farm buildings, Captain Schwartzwalder's men emerged, unexpected, to their right and effectively surrounded the Germans. The remaining Germans immediately surrendered and put out a white flag. However, as one of the Americans went forward to accept the surrender he was shot dead. It was, undoubtedly, the result of a nervous reflex reaction from one of the Germans as the men of the 82nd Airborne Division, to their credit, did not seek any revenge and took the remaining eight Germans prisoner.

For over eight hours a group of only twenty-eight German infantrymen[20] from the 1057 Grenadier Regiment, 91st Airlanding Division, had held out against hundreds of American troops. But the battle for la Fière Bridge had just begun and the 1/505 defended the bridge against several German counter-attacks down the causeway over the next few days.

Cauquigny

Walk down the causeway towards Cauquigny. As you cross la Fière Bridge you will notice that there is a sign on your right naming the lane voie Marcus Heim. Back in 1944 the area of low lying land on either side of the lane was extensively flooded, thereby turning the lane into a causeway. Farther along, also on the right, is a marker post that shows the level of the water on 6 June, 1944. Continue along the lane to Cauquigny and enter the church. Inside you will find a notice which briefly explains the importance of Cauquigny. If you return to the road and continue in a westward direction you will come to the junction which leads to Amfreville.

La Fiére causeway from Cauquigny end, down which the Germans launched their counter-attack.

Marker Post indicating height of the floods back in 1944.

The first counter-attack came later on the afternoon of D-Day. By this time the 505th PIR had dug in by the farm buildings and on either side of the road that led over the bridge and along the causeway to Cauquigny. On the west side of the floods, at Cauquigny, there were some men of Lieutenant-Colonel Charles Timmes's 2/507th PIR. They held the area around Cauquigny church and the fields and orchard to the north. After the farm buildings at la Fière had been taken Captain Schwartzwalder with some men from the 505th PIR were sent over to help reinforce the positions.

Captain Schwartzwalder wanted to push on and take Amfreville, but he first sought out Lt-Col Timmes in order to establish what the situation was in the area. Again the lack of communication equipment was to cause a major problem for the troops defending la Fière Causeway. The small groups scattered around both sides of the causeway had given the impression that the area was secure. But no one had any means of confirming this. Therefore, as Captain Schwartzwalder set off with his men to find Lt-Col Timmes, who was in a nearby orchard, the western side of the causeway around Cauquigny was left defended by only a handful of men.

It was just at that time that the Germans began their first counter-attack. In their defensive positions around Cauquigny church, Lieutenant Louis Levy and Lieutenant Joseph Kormylo, with only ten other men, prepared to defend their positions as the squealing and rumble of tank tracks was heard coming towards them. In an instant a German ambulance appeared at

91

La Fière bridge with Cauquigny in the distance.

the nearby road junction. It had paused for only a second while a Red Cross flag was waved before the vehicle disappeared out of sight in the direction of Amfreville (D126). The Germans, now aware of the American presence, fired five artillery shells at the road junction. These were followed by several more which landed along the river bank.

The small band of American paratroopers set up a machine-gun just behind the church which allowed them to cover the road. The rest of the men were spaced at 15 yard intervals and then sat tight waiting for the inevitable battle. The German tanks arrived at the intersection supported by infantry. Immediately the Americans opened fire on the German soldiers. Lieutenant Levy threw a grenade towards a machine-gun crew that were just setting up their gun and then withdrew to the churchyard. The German medium tank began shelling the church as more German infantry began firing and pushing their way through a nearby hedgerow.

From the churchyard the paratroopers realized they were too heavily outnumbered and so withdrew, heading for the orchards where Lt-Col Timmes and the rest of the men were.

But the battle at Cauquigny had not yet finished. Unknown to the others, a Private Orlin Stewart was still in his position as support for a bazooka team that had been set up as a road block.

Cauquigny Church.

However, the rest of the team had pulled out with Captain Schwartzwalder's men and Private Stewart, armed with a Browning Automatic Rifle (BAR) and some Gammon grenades, had been forgotten.

He had not seen what had happened as the tanks approached, but as soon as the tanks came into view Private Stewart saw the lead tank hit by an explosion and burst into flames. The source of the explosion was unknown but Private Stewart began running towards the other tanks with his Gammon bombs and Browning Automatic Rifle. Taking temporary shelter in a ditch he was soon joined by another private and a sergeant. These two troopers were also supplied with Gammon grenades, so as the next two tanks rolled forward Private Stewart gave the two paratroopers covering fire while they attacked the tanks with their grenades. The two old French Renault tanks[21] were disabled by the explosions and as one of the tank crews tried to escape their burning vehicle the sergeant threw a hand grenade which killed two, while Private Stewart shot the third with his gun.

Yet another medium tank appeared at the road junction and joined in the battle. The three men decided that they had done their fair share of the work that morning and made off in the direction of Lt-Col Timmes's group. The Germans had retaken the western exit of the causeway.

In the meantime, on the eastern side of the causeway, another road-block had been established. At this road-block the causeway was being held by four men with bazookas: Privates John D. Bolderson, Marcus Heim Jr., Lenold Peterson and Gordon Pryne.

There was also Private Clarence Becker with a machine-gun and a 57mm anti-tank gun, positioned about 150 yards from the bridge, on the high ground overlooking the causeway. To the south another two man bazooka team was in position as well as an unknown number of other men from Company A, 505th PIR, who were in the vicinity.

As an extra defence against an attack, the men had laid four anti-tank mines across the roadway about 30 yards along the causeway, in addition to an old broken down truck which was positioned across the causeway on the western side of the bridge. The causeway was also partially obscured by the trees that flanked either side of the road; trees that helped obscure any of Cauquigny from la Fière Bridge.

Later that afternoon the expected German counterattack came and three tanks approached round the bend in the road on the causeway. In support German infantry advanced alongside and behind the tanks. As the lead tank was approaching the mines and the tank commander looked out of his turret, Private Becker, on the left of the bazooka men opened up with his machine-gun and killed the German officer. The machine-gun fire was followed by four bazooka rockets fired by Privates Bolderson and Peterson.

The rockets appeared to have had no effect and the tank began returning fire. The air was now thick with the stench of cordite and other explosives as the battle heated up. Mortars, machine-gun and rifle fire created a deafening cacophony as the bazooka men positioned themselves to get a better field of fire.

We kept firing at the first tank until it was put out of action and on fire. The second tank came up and pushed the first tank out of the way. We moved forward toward the second tank and fired as fast as I could load the rockets in the bazooka. We kept firing at the second tank and we hit it in the turret where it is connected to the body.

Private Marcus Heim, 'A' Company, 505th PIR, 82nd Airborne Division

Private Peterson then fired a second shot which hit the tracks and then, running forward, managed to get a shot in the tank's rear which ruptured its fuel tank and it exploded into a ball of flames. Privates Heim and Peterson were nearly out of rockets now and so Heim ran back across the causeway to see if he could get any spare rockets from Privates Bolderson and Pryne. At this time the Company A Commander, Major Kellam, was killed by mortar fire while running towards the bridge with extra supplies of rockets.

Private Heim found a damaged bazooka lying on the ground and some rockets nearby. Managing to return to his comrade without being hit, the two men reloaded and continued firing at the tank. Also firing at the tank was the anti-tank gun positioned on the high-ground and soon the third tank was knocked out. With the loss of their armour the German infantry, who had been under constant fire from the rest of 'A' Company, began to withdraw. The causeway had been held and continued to be held during successive attacks on the following two days. For their part in the action each man in the four-man Bazooka team was recommended for, and awarded, the Distinguished Service Cross by their new Company Commander, Lieutenant John D. Dolan.

On D+3 Maj-Gen Ridgeway led an attack down the causeway to secure it once and for all. Brigadier-General Gavin was also there leading the attack with the 3/325th GIR, two companies, commanded by Captain Robert D. Rae, from 507 PIR and with supporting artillery fire provided by the 319th and 320th GFAB and 90th Infantry Division. Also with the infantry were elements of the 746th Tank Battalion.

At just after 10.00 hrs the attack began with a deafening artillery barrage. The battalion from the 325th GIR led the attack down the 500 yard causeway with the Sherman tanks in support. However, with the exception of a few burnt out German tanks, vehicles and trees, the causeway offered little protection from the withering German fire. Brig-Gen Gavin who was commanding the attack witnessed the gliderborne troops reach the west bank under the cover of an artillery barrage that was being laid down on the German positions.

Brig-Gen James M. Gavin.

It was then that one of the Sherman tanks made its way forward across the causeway, but as it began to manoeuvre around one of the wrecked German tanks it ran over a mine, ironically an American one which had been laid in the battle for la Fière Causeway on D-Day, and the explosion disabled the tank. The advance began to falter as men fell down dead or wounded. The assistant divisional commander gave the order for more troops to be sent into the maelstrom.

General Gavin came over to me and said 'Rae, you've got to keep going.' We came out shouting, forcing our way through the log-jam of dead and dying soldiers... We continued running until we reached the west bank.
Captain Robert D. Rae, 507th PIR, 82nd Airborne Division

95

On the west bank Captain Rae split his men into two sections, one to head south down the dirt road and help the 325th GIR, and the remaining section to continue with the push westward, however, more men were needed to reinforce the tenuous bridgehead. Maj-Gen Ridgeway had also gone down to the causeway now to urge his men on. Divisional and battalion commanders stood side by side with the other ranks on the causeway so that they could provide some inspiration to their men and continue with the attack.

We just grabbed our men and walked them out. The physical force of that fire pouring in was such that they just stopped and started back...[But] not from cowardice... We just grabbed them by the shoulders and led them down into this thing and pushed them. We were right there too.

Major-General Matthew B. Ridgeway, Commander 82nd Airborne Division

As the paratroopers pressed home their attack the men on the western bank of the floods were wondering where the armoured support was. Maj-Gen Ridgeway was also considering why the armour wasn't advancing. Instead of issuing orders though, the divisional commander made his way over to the causeway and saw that all the damaged armour now blocked the road for other tanks. Working alone he went over to the damaged Sherman and began feeding out a winching cable so that it could be used to pull the other wrecks to one side.

At the same time Brig-Gen Gavin was organising the tanks to prepare them for their crossing of the causeway. By midday the passage had been cleared and the tanks rolled forward across the causeway and towards the front line.

Cloth insignia of 325th Glider Infantry Regiment, 82nd Airborne Division.

With armour the infantry were able to exploit their bridgehead and the fighting continued amid the German artillery and mortar fire throughout the rest of the day and evening.

During the battle for la Fière Causeway there had been many heroic deeds performed by the men of the 82nd Airborne Division and also by those of other units and divisions that supported them. As with all battles many of these deeds went unnoticed and without reward, except for the self-satisfaction an individual gained from knowing he had helped his comrades. Some, though, would never know of any reward as

Some troops acquire their own transport.

The same spot today

their action would cost them their lives and only a few would receive any decoration for their valour.

One of those whose courage was witnessed, recorded and subsequently rewarded, however, was Private First Class Charles N. DeGlopper of 'C' Company, 325th GIR, 82nd Airborne Division. His company were one of the first to cross the causeway but when he realised that his platoon were in danger he selflessly sacrificed himself for his comrades. For this extreme valour he was awarded the United States highest award for gallantry. His citation tells the story:

Citation
MEDAL OF HONOR
PRIVATE FIRST CLASS CHARLES N. DEGLOPPER

He was a member of Company C, 325th Glider Infantry, on 9 June 1944 advancing with a forward platoon to secure a bridgehead across the Merderet River at la Fière, France. At dawn the platoon had penetrated an outer line of machine-guns and riflemen, but in so doing had become cut off from the rest of the company. Vastly superior forces began a decimation of the stricken unit and put in motion a flanking manoeuvre which would have completely exposed the American platoon in a shallow roadside ditch where it had taken cover. Detecting this danger, Pfc DeGlopper volunteered to support his comrades by fire from his automatic rifle while they attempted a withdrawal through a break in a hedgerow 40 yards to the rear. Scorning a concentration of enemy automatic weapons and rifle fire, he walked from the ditch onto the road in full view of the Germans, and sprayed the hostile positions with assault fire. He was wounded, but he continued firing. Struck again, he started to fall; and yet his grim determination and valiant fighting spirit could not be broken. Kneeling in the roadway, weakened by his grievous wounds, he levelled his heavy weapon against the enemy and fired burst after burst until killed outright. He was successful in drawing enemy action away from his fellow soldiers, who continued the fight from a more advantageous position and established the first bridgehead over the Merderet. In the area where he made his intrepid stand his comrades later found the ground strewn with dead Germans and many machine-guns and automatic weapons which he had knocked out of action. Pfc DeGlopper's gallant sacrifice and unflinching

Lt-Gen Omar Bradley awarding decorations after the battle for St Mère Eglise. Left; Brig-Gen. James Gavin, Lt-Col Krause, Lt-Col Vandervoort

Below Lt-Gen Omar Bradley decorating Lt-Col Krause (note the cane). Lt-Col Vandervoot is to his left.

heroism while facing insurmountable odds were in great measure responsible for the highly important tactical victory in the Normandy Campaign.

By the early hours of the 10 June, 1944 the bridgehead had been consolidated and the 2/357th Infantry Regiment, 90th Infantry Division were on their way to relieve the airborne troops and continue with the westward advance to cut off the Cotentin Peninsular. The 82nd division had succeeded in completing its main objective and now the battle for Normandy could continue.

1. op. cit. *Utah Beach to Cherbourg Report*.

2. op. cit. Andrews, John C. p.17.

3. Wills, Deryk. *Put on Your Boots and Parachutes!* (Private Publication, ISBN 0951845101. 1992). p.66.

4. Second Report of the Commanding General of the U.S. Army Air Forces to the Secretary of War (Published by US Government Printing Office, 1945). p.10.
(referred to hereafter as *The Arnold Report*).

5. Edwards, Commander Kenneth. *Operation Neptune*. (Collins, London, 1946). p.146.

6. Shilleto, Carl. *Pegasus Bridge/Merville Battery*. (Leo Cooper, Pen & Sword Book Ltd., Barnsley, 1999). p.43.

7. op. cit. *Utah Beach to Cherbourg Report*.

8. op. cit. Crookenden, Napier. pp.113 & 115.

9. op. cit. Blumentritt, Guenther. p.223.

10. op cit. Crookenden, Napier. P.113.

11. op. cit. Wills, Deryk. p.71.

12. Renaud, Alexandre, *Sainte-Mère-Église*. (Julliard, Paris, France, 1984). p.37.

13. op. cit Wills, Deryk. pp.71 & 73.

14. Keegan, John. *Six Armies in Normandy*. (Penguin Books Ltd., Harmondsworth, England, 1983). p.94.

15. op. cit. *Utah Beach to Cherbourg Report*.

16. op. cit. Crookenden, Napier. p.117.

17. ibid. p.118.

18. op. cit. Keegan, John. p.100.

19. op. cit. Crookenden, Napier. p.115.

20. Marshall, Brigadier-General S.L.A. *Night Drop*. (Little, Brown and Company, Boston, USA, 1962). P.62.

21. op. cit. Keegan, John. p.104.

CHAPTER FIVE

SECURING THE BRIDGEHEAD

Storming the Islands

Utah Beach is on the east side of the Cotentin Peninsular and can be reached by taking the **D70**, signposted St-Marie-du-Mont, off the **N13**, between Isigny-sur-Mer and St-Mère Église. From St-Marie-du-Mont take the **D913**, signposted Utah Beach and park in the car park in front of the Utah Beach Museum. Walk onto the beach by passing through the gap in the sand dunes to the left of the museum. This area was codenamed Exit 2 and is the place where the fifty-seven-year-old Brigadier-General Theodore Roosevelt landed on D-Day. To your right the museum is built on top of the former German gun emplacement which was known as W5. Look out to sea and to your left you will see, approximately four mile off-shore, the two small islands known as the Iles St Marcouf.

Just before 04.30 hrs, on D-Day, four scouts made their way, in rubber dinghies, to the shore of the Iles St Marcouf to mark the beach for an assault detachment from the 4th and 24th Cavalry Squadron. Aerial reconnaissance missions had shown enemy activity on the islands and so it was believed that the Germans may have installed a gun emplacement or observation post there. Therefore, in advance of the invasion fleet, Force 'U,' an assault force of some 132 men, commanded by Lieutenant E. C. Dunn, were tasked with attacking the islands prior to the main invasion on Utah Beach.

Bombing the Iles St Marcouf June 1944. This early morning raid was undoubtedly more successful than a similar raid on 'Omaha' Beach (where most of the bombs landed several miles inland). Even though the after-action report estimated that approximately one-third of the bombs dropped on 'Utah' Beach fell between the high and low tide water marks, most bombs did find their targets and the raid was considered a success. This undoubtedly contributed greatly to the success of the overall landings.

Rockets fired from an LCT (R). Below, LCVPs heading for the beaches at Utah.

Two waves of assault troops, divided between four LCAs (Landing Craft Assault), followed the scouts ashore. During the attack five men were killed by mines before they realized that there were no Germans occupying the islands.

By 05.30hrs[1] the islands had been taken, but during the course of the day the German booby-traps and mines accounted for another fourteen casualties. After the islands had been made safe a detachment of the 535th AAA Battalion occupied them while the two detachments of cavalry landed on Utah beach and went on to guard VII Corps Headquarters.[2]

The Beach Assault

As the Iles St Marcouf were being taken troops had already been transferred to their LCVPs (Landing Craft Vehicle Personnel). Also known as the 'Higgins Boat', after their designer, Andrew Higgins, they were not the favourite means of sea transport for the soldiers who had to endure the choppy seas of the English Channel. Only thirty-six foot long, and ten-and-a-half foot wide, the flat bottomed craft were prone to pitch and roll in the slightest of swells.

Fully laden, the small craft could transport thirty-six men or twelve men and a Jeep. To add to the discomfort of those aboard there was no seating space and the flat, blunt, bows of the craft ensured that everyone got a soaking as the landing craft powered through the rough sea.

An assortment of transport ships made up the invasion fleet on D-Day. Amongst them LSIs (Landing Ship Infantry) and LSTs (Landing Ship Tank) carried the troops and the smaller landing craft to a position about eleven miles off-shore. There the troops embarked their smaller landing craft and, accompanied by two pilot craft (PC 1176 and PC 1261) and four LCCs (Landing Craft Controls 60, 70, 80 & 90), were led to a point some 4,000 yards off-shore where the LCVPs would circle in the sea until given

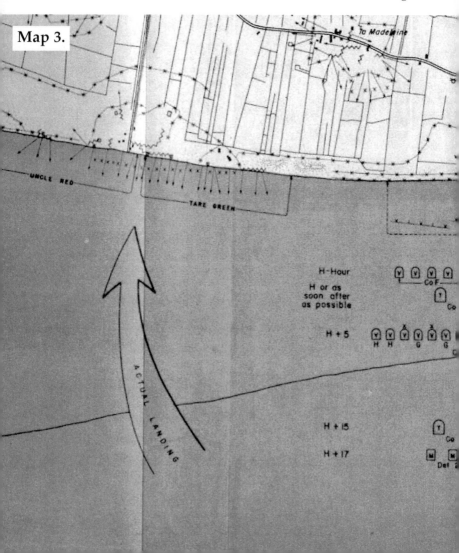

Map 3.

the order to head for the beach under escort.

The weather that morning was cloudy, with a westerly wind, and a surf of three to four feet.[3] By the time the troops boarded their landing craft many of them were eager to get onto solid ground. Force 'U' had the longest journey of all the assault forces and, combined with the twenty-four hour postponement of D-Day, this meant that some of the troops had been at sea for up to three nights and two days.

At 04.55 hrs[4] the landing craft were on their way towards Utah Beach. Twenty-four successive waves of landing craft would land on the beach over the next six hours. At 05.50 hrs the Allied warships began their bombardment of the German shore

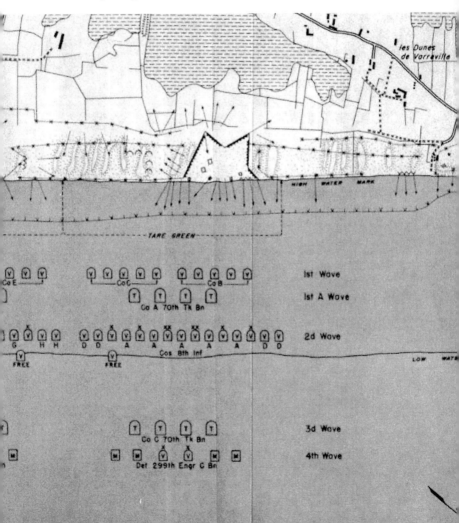

batteries and defences. Simultaneously, 276 Marauder medium bombers began dropping their payloads, a total of 4,404 250lb bombs, onto the German coastal positions.

As the LCVPs were heading for the two codenamed sections of Utah Beach, 'Uncle Red' and 'Tare Green,' so, too, were the eight LCTs (Landing Craft Tank). These landing craft each had on board four Duplex Drive Tanks, which should have been put into the sea some 5,000 yards off-shore. However, as the ships made their way to the shore PC 1261, which was guiding the two LCC vessels – LCC 80 AND LCC 90 – assigned to the 'Uncle Red' sector, hit a mine and began to sink.

> *I saw PC 1261 slowly rolling over and the stern went down fast. Neither I nor anyone else that was involved in the actual invasion could stop and pick them up. And this is the really sad part to go through, seeing these men screaming, hollering and asking for help. So now Red Beach doesn't have any control vessel at all, and that immediately set up a state of confusion. I mean these four LCTs with the DD tanks were going in all directions. They were only four boats, but they were trying to avoid running over the men who were in the water.*
> **Lieutenant Sims Gauthier, LCC 60.**

Within minutes there was another explosion as LCT 597 hit another mine and exploded. The landing craft sank within minutes taking her four Duplex Drive tanks with her. At this time it had been decided that the sea was too rough to allow the DD tanks to be launched so far from the shore so they were taken in to between 1,500 and 3,000 yards of the beach before they were discharged from the landing craft.

In the meantime the bombardment of Utah Beach continued. In addition to landing craft, thirty-two Sherman tanks, and thirty-seven self-propelled M-7 Priests, fired their guns onto the beach defences. Then, when the LCVPs were within 300 to 700 yards of the beach, a barrage of 1,064 five-inch rockets was fired from seventeen LCT(R)s that had been positioned some 3,000 yards off-shore. This final volley of explosive power drenched the beaches so that the first assault troops and tanks would have some clear passages through the German beach defences.

As the LCVPs carrying the assault troops neared the shore there was some confusion. A combination of the lost pilot craft, dust and debris obscuring the LCVP's observation of the shore, and a strong coastal current, resulted in the first waves landing several hundred yards south of their designated area.

The first wave ashore was twenty, thirty-man, assault teams from the 1/8th and 2/8th Infantry Regiment, 4th Infantry Division. Amongst them was Brigadier General Theodore Roosevelt, the Assistant Divisional Commander. Despite the heavy naval and aerial bombardment the men still came under artillery, small arms and mortar fire from the Germans.

I was with Company H of the 2nd Battalion and went in with the first wave of assault troops. Before we reached the shore something came through the side of our craft and tore quite a hole, in one side and out the other, tore a good size piece out of my backpack.

The history books say we landed some distance to the left than we were supposed to and that this was one of the easier landings. I don't know if this was good or bad. It did not seem good at the time. We went into the water somewhat more than waist deep and a good distance from dry land. When we came on shore we had a greeter, how he got there I do not know other than he was in one of the first landing craft, but Brigadier-General Theodore Roosevelt was standing there waving his cane and giving out instructions as only he could do. If we were afraid of the enemy, we were more afraid of him and could not have stopped on the beach had we wanted to.

Private Harper H. Coleman, 2/8th Infantry Regiment, 4th Infantry Division.

At 06.30 hrs the first assault teams, closely followed by the

remaining twenty-eight DD tanks stormed the beach.

Nearby stood the German strongpoint WN5. This German coastal gun emplacement was on the beach front and covered an area some 400 yards long and 300 yards deep. The troops defending WN5 were from the 3rd Company, 919th Grenadier Regiment, commanded by *Leutnant* Arthur Jahnke. Though only twenty-three-years-old *Leutnant* Jahnke was already a veteran of the Eastern Front and had been awarded the Knight's Cross for his actions, as a platoon leader, in the fight against the Russians. Despite his age Leutnant Jahnke had even won the respect of *Generalfeldmarschall* Rommel back on the 11 May,

German Strongpoint WN 5 with DD tanks of the 70th Tank Battalion on the beach in front of it, waiting for gaps to be made in the sea-wall. The house, Le Chalet Rouge, marks the northern end of WN 5; it still stands today.

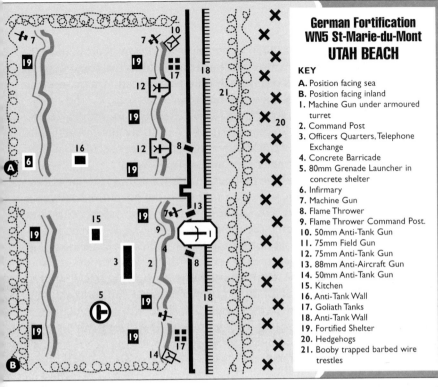

**German Fortification
WN5 St-Marie-du-Mont
UTAH BEACH**

KEY

A. Position facing sea
B. Position facing inland
1. Machine Gun under armoured turret
2. Command Post
3. Officers Quarters, Telephone Exchange
4. Concrete Barricade
5. 80mm Grenade Launcher in concrete shelter
6. Infirmary
7. Machine Gun
8. Flame Thrower
9. Flame Thrower Command Post.
10. 50mm Anti-Tank Gun
11. 75mm Field Gun
12. 75mm Anti-Tank Gun
13. 88mm Anti-Aircraft Gun
14. 50mm Anti-Tank Gun
15. Kitchen
16. Anti-Tank Wall
17. Goliath Tanks
18. Anti-Tank Wall
19. Fortified Shelter
20. Hedgehogs
21. Booby trapped barbed wire trestles

1944.[5] While on an inspection of the area Rommel had criticised the local commanders about the state of the beach defences, on hearing this *Leutnant* Jahnke protested and voiced his own opinion. In quick reply to Leutnant Jahnke's comments, *Generalfeldmarschall* Rommel had promptly asked to see the *Leutnant*'s hands. Young Jahnke, after first removing his gloves, showed his scratched and blistered hands to his superior. Suitably impressed by the evidence that at least one of his officers was physically doing his best to instal beach obstacles and gun positions, Rommel proceeded to congratulate *Leutnant* Jahnke on his efforts.

However, just after dawn, 6 June, 1944, WN 5 lay in ruins after an aerial attack. Most of the strongpoint's armaments were now either destroyed or damaged by the bombing raid. This was indistinguishable from shelling being put down by the sea-borne armada as it approached. Many of the German defenders

Leutnant **Arthur Jahnke.**

were in a state of shock as they appeared from their bunkers in the wake of the explosions. But worse was yet to come – as the dust and smoke began to clear the vast Allied armada became visible stretching across the horizon.

Leutnant Jahnke sent off a runner to the 122 mm battery, of the 1261st Artillery Regiment, situated at St-Martin-de-Varreville, with orders to lay down a barrage on the approaching landing craft. But the barrage never materialized.[6]

Within minutes the first landing craft belonging to the US 4th Infantry Division were grounding on the beach and lowering their ramps. The assault troops jumped into the surf and immediately began spreading out as they raced up the beach. For some, the effect of running through the cloying wet sand at the waters edge, fully laden with their equipment, was unsteadying and disorienting. The turbulent and long sea voyage having taken its toll on their senses. For most though, the adrenalin rush as they ran across the bomb and shell blasted sand towards the beach defences, was enough for them to forget the discomfort and misery of the past few days.

Just above the anti-tank wall, at WN 5, there was a German-manned French Renault tank that had been partially buried in

Utah Beach 6 June, 1944.

Leutnant Arthur Jahnke and his men of 3rd Coy 919th Grenadier Regiment.

the sand. Inside *Gefreiter* Friedrich began firing his machine-gun across the beach. The American troops dropped flat or dived for cover. Another machine-gun on the northern side of WN 5 also joined in. By this time the first wave was ashore and the men were making their way towards the relative protection the beach anti-tank wall provided. As the second wave landed so, too, did the DD tanks. The German machine-guns raked the beach and hit a leading group in the second wave.

The swiming DD tanks coming ashore at Utah were a shock for the Germans.

The Germans at WN 5 were also firing 80 mm mortar rounds out towards the vessels at sea. This, however, served only to give away the their position and a salvo of Allied naval artillery fire promptly silenced the mortars.

The Germans were also frantically trying to get their bomb-damaged 88 mm gun working. One shell was successfully loaded, and fired, which hit and disabled, but not completely destroy, one of the DD tanks. But, after the single round had been fired, the 88

111

Cloth insignia worn on left pocket by Engineer Special Brigade members.

Goliath tanks disarmed by Naval Engineers.

would not fire again and became just a useless piece of scrap iron.

The appearance of the floating DD tanks undoubtable surprised the German defenders, but the Germans also had their own unusual weapons. Known as the 'Goliath' tank, these were small, squat, compact tracked vehicles were operated by remote control. Packed with 224lbs of explosives they could also be detonated by the same remote control. *Leutnant* Jahnke ordered his men to send the Goliaths towards the American DD tanks. However, the Allied heavy bombardment had damaged the delicate electrical workings and the miniature tanks could not be controlled or deployed.

Along with the second wave the first of the engineers came ashore (1st Engineer Special Brigade) and were tasked with removing or destroying the beach obstacles. It was the engineers' initial task to clear eight, fifty yard wide, lanes on the beach. Helping them in this task would be a detachment of tank dozers from the 70th Tank Battalion and 612th Light Equipment Company.

Landing on the wrong part of the beach could, potentially,

have been disastrous for the seaborne forces and created even more confusion for the following waves. However, the assault force had the advantage that Brig-Gen Roosevelt was ashore and he quickly determined that the area where they had landed was less well defended than their original landing area. After consulting with his two battalion commanders, he gave the order that the following waves should be directed to where he had landed. As second-in-command of the US 4th Infantry Division he had the authority to redirect the landing forces to this sector and therefore the invasion continued without anyone attempting to countermand his orders. For his quick thinking and action on that day he was subsequently awarded the Medal of Honor:

Citation
MEDAL OF HONOR
BRIGADIER-GENERAL THEODORE ROOSEVELT

For gallantry and intrepidity at the risk of his life above and beyond the call of duty on 6 June 1944, in France, after two verbal requests to accompany the leading assault elements in the Normandy invasion had been denied. Brigadier General Roosevelt's written request for this mission was approved and he landed with the first wave of the forces assaulting the enemy-held beaches. He repeatedly led groups from the beaches, over the sea wall and established them inland. His valour, courage and

Brig-Gen Theodore Roosevelt Jr. (left), 4th Inf. Div. Asst Commander; Major-Gen Raymond Barton (middle), 4th Inf. Div. Commander; Lt-Col Huffer (right), 746th Tank Bn, confer in the dunes on Utah.

presence in the very front of the attack and his complete unconcern at being under heavy fire inspired the troops to heights of enthusiasm and self-sacrifice. Although the enemy had the beach under constant direct fire, Brigadier-General Roosevelt moved from one locality to another, rallying men around him, directed and personally led them against the enemy. Under his seasoned, precise, calm and unfaltering leadership, assault troops reduced beach strongpoints and rapidly moved inland with the minimum casualties. He thus contributed substantially to the successful establishment of the beachhead in France.

For many troops though the experience of battle was a confusing and harrowing experience, particularly for those who were experiencing it for the first time. Nevertheless, their instinct for survival would force them to learn quickly the hard lessons of war:

I was wearing my lifebelt cowboy style instead of round my chest. I was in the front, standing next to a guy from the Navy. The front of the boat opened up and the sailor jumped into the water which was up to his shoulders. In England we were told that we would be in ankle deep water so I yelled that they should bring the boat in closer to shore. Someone behind me pushed me and my lifebelt inflated as I fell into the water. Guys were jumping into the water heading into battle, and I was floating on my back. One of my buddies grabbed my foot and towed me in to the beach. I saw a sign at the edge of the water that had a drawing of a skull and crossbones and it said "Achtung Minen." Shells were landing on the beach and in the water and someone clutching his shoulder was yelling "Medic..." I was crawling on the beach and a Major asked me if I was wounded. I told him I wasn't but every time I got up, everyone else hit the ground. Every time I hit the ground, everyone else got up. Since this was happening several times a minute, I just stayed down. He gave the following advice..."When you hear bang, followed by a whistle, that's our stuff and you don't have to hit the ground, but when you hear a whistle before a bang, that's the time to take cover." Then he hit the ground and pulled me down with him. After that, I practised his advice successfully for the next seven months.

Private First Class Arthur L. Herzberg, Company A, 359th Infantry Regiment, 90th Infantry Division.

In the meantime the continued naval artillery barrage on W5

The beaches are secured.

eventually proved too much for the German defenders, and finally the strongpoint was overrun. *Leutnant* Jahnke, and those men of his company who survived, were taken prisoner and grouped on the beach to await a transfer to the Allied ships. However, artillery fire continued to land on Utah Beach, from German batteries along the Cotentin Peninsular, throughout the landings and for

German prisoners are processed on the beach.

Soldiers digging in and re-organizing on Utah Beach.

many days afterwards (the last reported artillery fire being on D+13).

Throughout the morning the infantry moved forward across the beach and on towards the causeways to establish contact with the airborne troops. In the meantime the engineers began the painstaking job of securing the beach and clearing it of mines for the following waves of troops. Amongst the many troops who engaged in the hazardous task of beach clearing was Sergeant Joseph Z. Pritchett, Jr., 531st Engineer Shore Regiment. Just one of the many engineers whose work, carefully clearing and disarming mines and booby-traps, would continue for several weeks.

Throughout the morning the engineers of the 531st ESB had experienced problems when one of their landing craft, carrying bulldozers and other equipment, hit an off-shore mine and sank. While another of the engineers' LCTs attempted to land on the beach, it came under fire from one of the German batteries, which cost the regiment one of its men and two more bulldozers.

The task of clearing the minefields though would last for weeks and throughout this time the toll for the engineers would steadily grow. By the end of the first day alone the engineers of the 1st ESB had suffered some 107 casualties, twenty-one of whom were killed.[7]

Another of the engineers who landed, and performed his tasks dutifully, on D-Day was Colonel Eugene M. Caffey, deputy commander of the 1st Engineer Special Brigade. Colonel Caffey had been the commander of the 1st ESB until the 9 May, 1944. However, because of the 1st ESB's performance during Exercise Tiger, Lt-Gen Bradley decided (apparently unaware of the extent of the losses the engineers suffered during the E-boat attack) that there had been a breakdown in the organisation structure of the 1st ESB and that Colonel Caffey should be relieved of his command. Therefore Major-General Collins assigned Brigadier-General James E. Wharton as the new brigade commander. Fortunately, in a twist of fate, Colonel Caffey was kept on as deputy commander and allowed to continue running the brigade as he always had done.

Colonel Caffey did not find out until after the war, when he read Lt-Gen Bradley's memoirs *A Soldier's Story*, that the First Army Commander was unaware of the major tragedy off

German casualties at W5.

Slapton Sands at the time and of the effect that it may have had on the exercise.[8]

Nevertheless Colonel Caffey still performed his tasks with great devotion and was subsequently awarded the following citation for his efforts on D-Day:

Citation
COLONEL EUGENE M. CAFFEY

Colonel Eugene M. Caffey (Army Serial No 09329), Corps of Engineers, United States Army, for extraordinary heroism in connection with military operations against an armed enemy on 6 June 1944, in France. Colonel Caffey landed with the first wave [sic] *of the forces assaulting the enemy-held beaches. Finding that the landing had been made on other than the*

planned beaches he selected appropriate landing beaches, redistributed the area assigned to shore parties of the 1st Engineer Special Brigade, and set them at work to establish routes inland through the sea wall and minefields to reinsure the rapid landing and passage inshore of the following waves. He frequently went on the beaches under heavy shellfire to force incoming troops to disperse and move promptly off the shore and away from the water side to places of concealment and greater safety further back. His courage and his presence in the very front of the attack, coupled with his calm disregard of hostile fire, inspired the troops to heights of enthusiasm and self-sacrifice. Under his experienced and unfaltering leadership, the initial error in landing off-course was promptly overcome, confusion was prevented, and the forces necessary to a victorious assault were successfully and expeditiously landed and cleared from the beaches with a minimum of casualties. He thus contributed, in a marked degree, to the seizing of the beachhead in France.

Colonel Eugene Caffey on Utah Beach June 1944.

Colonel Caffey was also further rewarded by once again being given the command of the 1st ESB, on the 2 July, 1944, when Brig-Gen Wharton was made assistant commander of the 9th Infantry Division.

Colonel Caffey also raised the first Stars and Stripes over Utah Beach, where it remained until November, 1944, when the beach was finally closed down (the flag is now in the Utah Beach Museum). During the five months that Utah Beach was operational, and used for landing and loading material and men, some 750,000 tons of supplies, 200,000 vehicles and guns, and 40 per cent of all the troops that landed in Normandy went across Utah Beach. It was across this same beach that some 40,000 wounded troops and 60,000 German prisoners were also evacuated.[9]

Cloth insignia of Advance Section (ADSEC) which dealt with logistics for Engineer Special Brigades.

But it was not just the officers that were committed to their tasks, so too, were many of the other ranks, the ordinary soldier, sailor and airman. Many histories overlook the contribution made by so many different units during the Normandy campaign, concentrating instead on just the heroic actions of the men fighting the battle on the front line. But without the support and assistance given by the wide variety of services, the soldier at the front would not be able to receive his supplies, ammunition or food. Perhaps the most fitting tribute to one of these groups, the engineers, is in the comment made by a naval officer after the landings. Inter-service rivalry forgotten, he said:

The efficiency and smoothness with which the landing was

1st Engineer Special Brigade.

Sgt Joseph Pritchett 531st ESR, killed in action 25 June, 1944.

Road marker to the memory of Sgt. JZ Pritchett.

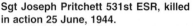

made and the operation of the beaches carried on were stated not to have been surpassed anywhere. Much of the credit for the success of the operation is due the 1st Engineer Special Brigade and the 531st Engineer Shore Regiment which was a component of it. Brigade and regimental Commands not only had the knowledge, skill and experience necessary to successfully carry-on the operation but, as well, consistently were motivated by a spirit of co-operation and help, which did much to facilitate the performance of duty by the Navy. The thanks of the 2nd Beach Battalion are extended for that co-operation.[10]

Commander Curtain, 2nd Naval Beach Battalion.

For the engineers that lost their lives during those first vital weeks of the Normandy landings, the roadways leading to and from Utah Beach have since been named in their honour. Amongst the many names commemorated on the roadside plaques is that of Sergeant J. Z. Pritchett, Jr., who was killed on the 25 June while removing anti-personnel mines in a bivouac area just off the 'Roger White' sector of Utah Beach.

The loss of equipment and men was a constant problem for the commanders, and particulary for the troops that were coming ashore and pushing onto the front to fight. In some cases it was a matter of having to distribute stores and rations far wider than had been anticipated.

One noteworthy event that happened that afternoon, it may have been the next afternoon, but I think it was D-Day afternoon... Anyway Lt-Gen Omar Bradley came to our command post...he'd come to our headquarters to notify us that one of the battalions of the 9th Infantry Division was part of the floating reserve and that their ship had been sunk out from under them in the Channel. These troops were coming ashore wet. without weapons and without ammunition. We were to post signs at the beach exits and create a little dump there where the other troops coming ashore could throw down some ammunition for the soldiers of the 9th Division... you never hear much about that, I never heard much about it, but I do know I sent a message to 531st Engineers on the beach.
Captain Sam Daugherty, 1st Engineer Special Brigade HQ.

Medics treating the casualties.

4th Inf Div. personnel crossing over the flooded land beyond Utah Beach.

Despite the problems encountered on the beach, and out at sea, in total, on D-Day alone, over 20,000 troops manage to land on Utah Beach along with some 1,700 vehicles.[11] The casualty figure on that day, for the 4th Infantry Division as a whole, has been put at 197 (though some secondary sources put this figure at just over 200) men, including 60 who were lost at sea. Because of the inevitable confusion caused during the heat of battle it is difficult, if not impossible, for accurate figures to be determined. However, because the Utah Beach casualties were relatively light, in comparison to the other beach landings and the airborne drops, these figures are undoubtedly the most accurate of all the landing areas.

The fighting on the beach itself began to wane around midday, inland though, the battle for the beachhead continued and the next task for the 4th Infantry Division was to establish contact with the 101st and then the 82nd Airborne Division.

The Airborne Linchpin

From Utah Beach take the **D913** back through St Marie-du-Mont across the **N13** towards Carentan. To find la Barquette and le Port take the old Highway 13 into Carentan and follow local signposts (a local map can also be obtained from the local Tourist Information Office which is situated and signposted along this road). From Carentan return to St Marie-du-Mont along the **D913** and continue towards Utah Beach. At the next crossroads turn right (south-east) onto the **D115** and head towards le Grand Vey. Take the next left, onto the **D329**, and this will take you to Pouppeville (Exit 1). From Pouppeville return to the crossroads along the **D115** and turn right onto the **D913**, signposted Utah Beach, and this will take you to Haudienville (Exit 2).

From Haudienville take the D913 back to St Marie-du-Mont and then take the first right turn onto the D70. Take the next turning left, onto the D329, and this will take you to Hiesville (LZ 'E').

The 101st Airborne Division provided the linchpin that would hold the Allied bridgehead together on the Cotentin Peninsular. While the 82nd Airborne Division fought to establish the west and north-west of the bridgehead around St Mère Église, and the 4th Infantry Division secured the beach to the east, the 101st Airborne division was tasked with securing the area in between and with protecting the northern and southern flanks.

To the south, near DZ 'D', Colonel Howard Johnson the commander of the 501st PIR, managed to gather some 145 men together after their drop and went on to secure their main objective which was the lock at la Barquette. However, an initial attempt to move towards the railway and road bridges over the River Douve, upstream and north of Carentan, with the intention of destroying them, was soon thwarted when their advance drew heavy enemy fire. Instead of continuing the attack on the River Douve bridges, Colonel Johnson decided that it was more important to hold the area around the la Barquette lock. Throughout the morning more paratroopers joined Colonel Johnson's force, and so an attempt was then made to move towards the village of la Basse Addeville and St Côme-du-Mont. However, Colonel Johnson's force again proved too small and the German resistance in this area too heavy.

The 3/506th PIR were also to land on DZ 'D' (along with

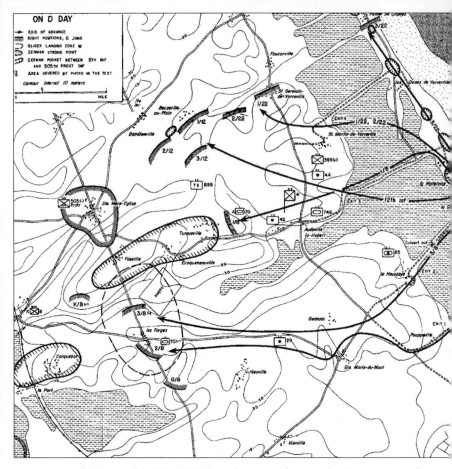

1/501st and 2/501st PIR) and secure the two bridges across the
River Douve at le Port. These were initially taken but an
adequate bridgehead could not be established because of
German resistance.

Farther north the 1/506th and 2/506th PIR landed mainly
around St Marie-du-Mont, DZ 'C', and were tasked with
securing the area around the western side of the causeway's
Exits 1 and 2. Only ten sticks managed to land on the drop zone,
but of those that landed nearby one included the 101st Airborne
Division's Commander Major General Maxwell Taylor. In fact
the drop was his first combat jump and only the fifth parachute
jump that Maj-Gen Taylor had ever made and a jump that
finally qualified him for his parachute wings.[12]

After a good landing in a field near St Marie-du-Mont, Maj-
Gen Taylor moved off to find more of his men. By chance he,

literally, bumped into his Artillery Commander, Brigadier-General Anthony C. McAuliffe. As daylight approached more men had gathered, including the division's Chief of Staff Colonel Gerald J. Higgins. The officers recognized where they were from the distinct shape of the church tower at St Marie-du-Mont. After some discussion with his chief-of-staff, Maj-Gen Taylor concluded that the parachute drops had not gone to plan. Nevertheless, he decided that they must give the 4th Infantry Division as much help as was possible under the circumstances. After issuing his orders to those gathered, he added with dry humour:

Never in the history of military operations have so few been commanded by so many.
Major-General Maxwell D. Taylor, Commander, 82nd A/B Division.

Colonel Sink, commander of the 506th PIR, had managed to collect some forty men from his headquarters staff and met Lieutenant-Colonel William L. Turner, commander of the 1/506th PIR. Together they went to the objective at Culoville (Caloville on IGN map 1311 E) without meeting any opposition. From his command post Colonel Sink sent off patrols to reconnoitre the nearby villages of Vierville and St Marie-du-Mont while Lt-Col Turner was sent off to seize the causeway, Exit 1, at Pouppeville.

At the same time Lieutenant-Colonel Robert L. Strayer, and some of his men from the 2/506th PIR, were making their way towards their objective, Exit 2. Having landed in the vicinity of DZ 'A' it took a while for the men to get orientated and make their journey to Exit 2. After several skirmishes and having to by-pass a German battery on the way they finally arrived at Exit 2, at Haudienville, at around midday. There they found that there were no Germans guarding the causeway.

The 3/501st PIR were also to land on DZ 'C' and were tasked with securing the area around Landing Zone 'E' for the glider landings. They would then be used as a reserve battalion for any other operations. However, because of the confusion Maj-Gen Taylor ordered the 3/501st commander, Lt-Col Julian Ewell, to take Exit 1 at Pouppeville. Like Exit 2, this was secured around midday (before Lt-Col Turner and his men arrived) and contact was soon established with the 4th Infantry division from Utah Beach.

It was the following day when the action intensified near St Côme-du-Mont, along the road at Beaumont (D913), that just one of many of the tragedies experienced during the Normandy landings, began. This was when Lt-Col Turner mounted one of the tanks of the 70th Tank Battalion to give firing directions to the tank commander. Within a few seconds a sniper's bullet went through his head and the battalion commander slumped to the ground.

Silver parachute wings.

The loss for one American family was further intensified, less than seven weeks later, when Lt-Col William Turner's younger brother, First Lieutenant Dennis T. Turner, Jr., was also killed in action. The two brothers now rest, side by side, in the grounds of the Normandy American Military Cemetery and Memorial*** (see Appendix C).

The glider landings of the 101st Airborne Division (Operation 'Chicago') took place around 04.00 hrs. Of the fifty-two Waco gliders that set of from Aldermaston, England, fifty-one managed to make the air space over the Cotentin Peninsular, one having broken its tow rope over England and returned to the airfield at Aldermaston. Unfortunately this glider happened to contain the only long-range radio set – SCR 499 – which Maj-Gen Taylor was going to use to establish contact with its base in Berkshire[14].

The remaining fifty-one gliders flew over the Cotentin but came under heavy anti-aircraft fire. One glider, and its tow, was shot down over Pont l'Abbe and another pilot lost his way and released his glider south of Carentan. Another twenty-two gliders were hit by ground fire but still managed make their way towards the landing zone. There was also an additional problem for the glider pilots, one which came about as a result of ignoring Air Chief Marshal Sir Leigh-Mallory's recommendation that the gliders should land after dawn:

It was pitch black... We were supposed to have had moon, but when we got over Normandy there was no moon. In fact, the whole formation flew into a low cloud bank and split up, and we were never able to get back together again to make a concentrated landing. When we cut loose you couldn't see a blessed thing,

---

***As a reminder of the loss experienced by some American families as a result of the Normandy Campaign there are some thirty-eight pairs of brothers buried, side by side, in the Normandy American Military Cemetery. Perhaps most poignant of all though, is the father and son that are buried next to each other.

that's the scary part. You know that you have to come down, but you don't know what's down there...you can't see the fields or trees, you couldn't see anything 'til the darn last minute. I landed on a beautiful field that had a huge ditch across the middle, which we didn't know was there, and when we hit it, we broke the back of the glider. I was probably going about seventy-five miles an hour.'

George Buckley, Glider Pilot, 434th Troop Carrier Group, USAAF.

Cloth garrison cap badges.

Glider pilot George Buckley had landed his glider about a quarter of a mile from the landing zone. But not everyone was so lucky as he was and survived the crash landing. Only six of the forty-nine gliders managed to land in the landing zone, while another fifteen landed within half-a-mile. The rest landed within a couple of miles of the landing zone, with ten landing in a group near les Forges.

The first fatal casualty in the gliders occurred when the lead glider, which had been nicknamed 'The Flying Falcon,' landed in a field near Hiesville (D329). On board was the Assistant Divisional Commander, of the 101st Airborne Division, Brigadier-General Don F. Pratt. Flying the glider was an experienced pilot Lieutenant-Colonel Mike Murphy; however, on landing the glider skidded across the damp grass and crashed into an hedgerow. Various accounts continue to be given as to the exact circumstances in which Brig-Gen Pratt met his death. What is certainly true is that his death was caused by a fracture to his vertebrae.

There are, however, some discrepancies in accounts that have been given as to how Brig-Gen Pratt was killed during his flight to Normandy. Arlington National Cemetery Records, Washington DC, (where Brig-Gen Pratt in now buried) says that he was seated next to the pilot Lt-Col Murphy and was killed when the jeep the glider was carrying broke loose on impact and crushed the general. Other sources claim that the glider had special armour plating fitted beneath where the general was to be seated, for his safety, and that this affected the trim of the glider during its decent. The result was that the glider spun out

The glider, 'The Flying Falcon', in which Brig-Gen. Don F Pratt was killed.

of control and crashed.

The most popular claim, however, is made by the 101st A/B Division historian Mark A. Bando. He concludes that Brig-Gen Pratt had been restrained in a jeep, in the rear of the glider, and that he had been seated on a parachute. This sufficiently raised his head high enough so that the impact of landing caused his skull to smash against one of the overhead support structures in the glider, thereby breaking his neck.[15]

Whatever the true reason, Brig-Gen Pratt still became the first Allied General to be killed in the Normandy Campaign. His pilot, Lt-Col Murphy, survived the crash but suffered a broken leg. Of all the glider landings in this area some seventeen American troops were injured, four more were killed and seven were taken prisoner.[16]

The Northern Causeways[17]

Retrace your route back to St Marie-du-Mont and drive towards Utah Beach on the D913. Take the next left turn, at the crossroads, onto the D14 and drive due north-west towards St Germain-de-Varreville. At the crossroads with the D423 there is St Martin-de-Varreville to your right (east) and les Mézières to your left (west). By continuing north along the road you will reach Foucarville after passing through St Germain-de-Varreville.

To the north the 502nd PIR landed around DZ 'A,' but they suffered the worst parachute drop of all the parachute regiments.

Over half of the 2/502nd PIR were dropped on the wrong DZ landing around DZ 'C.' To make matters worse, their commanding officer, Lieutenant-Colonel Steve Chappuis, suffered an injured leg on landing. Nevertheless, Lt-Col Chappuis collected a dozen of his men and continued towards his objective, the 122 mm German gun Battery at St Martin-de-Varreville.

Insignia of the 502nd Parachute Infantry Regiment.

At this point Lt-Col Chappuis had a change of fortune. On arriving at the German battery he discovered that the area had been vacated having already received a particularly heavy pounding from the aerial bombardment. Satisfied that there were no Germans about the men dug in and waited for stragglers to join them.

Lieutenant-Colonel Robert E. Cole, commander of the 3/502nd PIR, had landed near St Mère Église. Disorientated by his drop Lt-Col Cole wasted over an hour travelling in the wrong direction. Eventually he knocked on a door of a house they came across and was told by a local women that they were in St Mère Église. The men immediately moved off in the right direction, gathering more lost paratroopers on the way. At one point they ran into a German patrol but the paratroopers managed to overpower them.

By the time Lt-Col Cole had neared his objective, with a now ever growing band of soldiers made up from men of nearly every parachute unit that had dropped that morning, he was informed that Lt-Col Chappuis had taken the battery at St Martin- de-Varreville.

Lt-Col Cole then decided to spilt his force, now numbering some eighty men, into two groups sending one to secure the causeway, Exit 3, while he led the rest of the men to Exit 4. The two causeways were then secured without a fight and his men were dug in by 07.30 hrs. Lt-Col Cole was frustrated at not having been involved in more of a fight with the Germans. As the morning went by and the 4th Infantry division began pushing inland some Germans began retreating along the causeways. But the paratroopers, without suffering any casualties, were easily able to pick off the Germans as they retreated.

If Lt-Col Cole was spoiling for a fight, he didn't have long to wait. Five days later the 101st Airborne Division had to fight their way along the main road, and over four bridges, into Carentan (Highway 13). In an epic battle which took place over the fourth bridge in an area known as 'The Cabbage Patch', Lt-Cole had his moment of glory. For his gallant effort he was subsequently awarded the 101st Airborne Division's first Medal of Honor. His citation says all that needs to be said:

Citation
MEDAL OF HONOR
LIEUTENANT-COLONEL ROBERT G. COLE

Lt. Col. Cole was personally leading his battalion in forcing the last 4 bridges on the road to Carentan when his entire unit was suddenly pinned to the ground by intense and withering enemy rifle, machine-gun, mortar, and artillery fire placed upon them from well prepared and heavily fortified positions within 150 yards of the foremost elements. After the devastating and unceasing enemy fire had for over 1 hour prevented any move and inflicted numerous casualties, Lt. Col. Cole, observing this almost hopeless situation, courageously issued orders to assault the enemy positions with fixed bayonets. With utter disregard for his own safety and completely ignoring the enemy fire, he rose to his feet in front of his battalion and with drawn pistol shouted to his men to follow him in the assault. Catching up a fallen man's rifle and bayonet, he charged on and led the remnants of his battalion across the bullet-swept open ground and into the enemy position. His heroic and valiant action in so inspiring his men resulted in the complete establishment of our bridgehead across the Douve River. The cool fearlessness, personal bravery, and outstanding leadership displayed by Lt. Col. Cole reflect great credit upon himself and are worthy of the highest praise in military service.

Unfortunately, Lt-Col Cole would never learn of his award. On the 18 September, 1944, during Operation 'Market Garden' Lt-Col Cole was shot dead by a German sniper.

The final task for the 502nd PIR was for the 1/502nd PIR, commanded by Lieutenant-Colonel Patrick J. Cassidy, to secure defensive positions to the north, around Foucarville. In addition there was also a German artillery barracks at les Mézières, near St Martin-de-Varreville to be taken. This objective had been codenamed 'WXYZ.'

While making his way towards St Martin-de-Varreville, Lt-Col Cassidy met Captain Lillyman, from the Pathfinders, who informed him that the battery at St Martin-de-Varreville was empty. Captain Lillyman was then ordered to go and establish a road-block to the North of Foucarville and Lt-Col Cassidy continued to les Mézières and set up his command post in one of the houses there. He then gave orders for a patrol, led by Sergeant Snyder, to check on how Lt-Col Cole's 3/502nd was doing at Exit 4, and for Staff-Sergeant Harrison Summers to take fifteen men and clear the nearby German artillery barracks.

When Staff-Sergeant Summers set off he was about to undertake a mission that would later be considered one of the most remarkable feats of endurance, skill, and determination, recorded during the Normandy Campaign. The group of men walked towards their object with Staff-Sergeant Summers in the lead. The artillery barracks in question was not a formal military installation but a series of farmhouses that had been requisitioned by the Germans and adapted for their use. In total there were some eleven buildings that were situated on both sides of the road (D423) that went through les Mézières. Farther east (across the D14) was the German battery, held by Lt-Col Chappuis.

The small patrol consisted of men from various units, none of whom were familiar to Staff-Sergeant Summers. Since the group appeared not to be particularly interested in the task Staff-Sergeant Summers decided to lead by example rather than issuing orders, hoping that the group would follow him into action.

As they neared their objective Staff-Sergeant Summers charged the first building, kicked the door open, and fired his Tommy gun. Four of the German soldiers fell dead while the rest beat a hasty retreat through a back door. Outside not a single

131

Carentan railway line after fighting by 101st A/B Division...

and the railway as it looks today.

paratrooper followed. Most of the other paratroopers now took cover in the nearby road ditch, their only contribution being some covering fire. Staff-Sergeant Summers charged across the road and forced his way into the second building only to find that the Germans had gone.

At this point Private William A. Burt had moved forward and set up his machine-gun in front of the second building. Firing at the third building, from which the Germans had now started to fire their own weapons, the private was able to force the Germans to take cover long enough for Staff-Sergeant Summers to kick open the door to this building and charge inside. This time Lieutenant Elmer F. Brandenberger had joined the group and charged the third building with the Staff-Sergeant; however, there was an explosion next to Lieutenant Brandenberger as he charged the building and the blast shattered his arm as he fell to the ground. Staff-Sergeant Summers nevertheless continued, entered the third building, and mowed down six more German soldiers. Outside Lieutenant Brandenberger was taken away for medical assistance.

Staff-Sergeant Summers rested for about half-an-hour, but before he set off to tackle the fourth building, an unidentified captain, from the 82nd Airborne Division, joined him and both men charged the next building. The captain was shot through the heart by a sniper and fell before they reached the door. Once again the door was kicked in and the occupants were swiftly dealt with by the Staff-Sergeant's Tommy gun. Some of the Germans, who had fled through a back door surrendered to the American paratroopers in the nearby ditch.

Private John Camin now decided to join Summers and with covering fire provided by Private Burt at the machine-gun the two paratroopers stormed another five farm buildings. On each occasion all the Germans inside were killed, some thirty in total. The ninth building was larger than the rest and when Staff-Sergeant Summers kicked the door open he found to his surprise that some fifteen Germans were seated in a mess hall, seemingly oblivious to all the fighting going on around them, and eating their breakfast. Summers kept up his momentum, as to stop and take prisoners would take-up precious time and give the remaining Germans time to counterattack. So all were shot where they sat.

The final building was used by the Germans as the main barracks and was a large two-storey, structure. The group of paratroopers in the ditch moved along towards the building which was set back in a field and obscured by a hedgerow and bank beside the road. As the paratroopers approached a German sniper opened fire hitting several American troops. The paratroopers in the ditch finally decided to make a break for it and charged through the hedgerow and across the seventy-five yard stretch of open ground towards the building. The Germans were quick to respond and opened fire on the group. Eight paratroopers fell, four dead, and the rest beat a hasty retreat to the roadside.

Private Burt fired his machine-gun at a nearby haystack which immediately caught fire. As the fire took hold, ammunition in a shed next to the haystack began to explode. About thirty Germans came running out of the shed to escape the blaze and all were shot as they ran across the open ground. The Germans in the barrack building though were unmoved.

The group was now joined by Staff-Sergeant Roy Nickrent who had appeared with a bazooka. After firing six shots into the roof of the barrack building the top storey was set ablaze. All the American paratroopers now concentrated their fire on the building. Soon the Germans began to flee from the barracks. Some fifty were shot down as they ran away while the few that escaped were rounded-up later.

At 15.30 hrs the battle for the barracks known as 'WXYZ' was finally over. It had lasted some five hours, during which time the airborne and seaborne troops had linked-up and were now establishing a firm foothold on the Cotentin Peninsular. Throughout the attack on the barracks, Staff-Sergeant Summers had continued with his assault with a total disregard for his own safety and with a selfless determination to do his job as best he could.

Some would have thought Staff-Sergeant Summers deserved the Medal of Honor; however, for some reason the powers-that-be considered that for his action Staff-Sergeant Summers would instead receive a Distinguished Service Cross. Later he received a battlefield commission.[18] This is a clear reminder that even those whose actions are witnessed and recorded are not necessarily going to be justly rewarded in the fickle, and sometimes unjust, system of awards.

Conclusion

By the end of D-Day the 101st Airborne Division had accomplished its most important tasks. To the north, the area around Foucarville was being held, and to the south, the lock at la Barquette and much of the area around St Côme-du-Mont was also in American hands. However, the American airborne troops were below strength and were unable to establish themselves a bridgehead over the River Douve. Between St Mére Église and Utah Beach though, the 101st Airborne Division had successfully secured the causeways for the seaborne troops.

To the west, the bridgehead was held tenuously around la Fière because of communication problems and also, like the 101st Airborne Division, as a result of their severely reduced forces they were unable to establish a sizeable bridgehead over the River Merderet. However, St Mère Église was firmly in the hands of the 82nd Airborne Division and therefore they had achieved their main objective.

The successful landings on Utah Beach to the east allowed the seaborne troops to move swiftly inland and reinforce the paratroopers with men, supplies and armour. However, as a result of heavy German resistance, VII Corps were unable achieve all their objectives as scheduled. In addition to men and

The terrible cost of war on the civillians of Normandy.

resources being rescheduled and diverted to help the airborne units, there were also problems with the unloading of supplies and men on Utah Beach. Because of continued artillery fire that was hitting the beach from German batteries, by the second day of the landings the Americans were already behind schedule. Instead of the planned total of 39,722 men, 4,732 vehicles, and 7,000 tons of supplies that should have been landed at Utah Beach; they had only managed to land 32,000 men, 3,200 vehicles and 2,500 tons of supplies.[19]

The lack of equipment and supplies, combined with the continued and sustained resistance by the German troops in the area, would ensure that the American would have a bitter and costly fight in the weeks ahead. That final objective, of securing the Cotentin Peninsular and capturing the port of Cherbourg, was not to be completed until the 1 July, 1944. Only then did the last of the German defenders around Cherbourg capitulate and the Allies finally gained complete control of the Cotentin Peninsular.

1. op. cit. *Utah Beach to Cherbourg Report*. p.43.
2. Cawne, Jonathan. *Spearheading D-Day*. (Histoire & Collections, Paris, France, 1998). p.68.
3. op. cit. Edwards, Commander Kenneth. p.146.
4. Howarth, David. *Dawn of D-Day*. (Odhams, Watford, England, 1959). p.115.
5. Carell, Paul. *Invasion They're Coming*. (E.P. Dutton & Co., Ltd., London, England 1973) p.28.
6. ibid. pp.56 & 57.
7. op. cit. Berger, Sid. p.226.
8. ibid. pp.97,235 & 236
9. op. cit. Devoe, Howard G. p.20.
10. op. cit. Berger, Sid. p.227.
11. op. cit. *Utah Beach to Cherbourg Report*. p.55.
12. op. cit. Crookenden, Napier. p.97.
13. op. cit. Marshall, Brigadier General S.L.A.. p.271.
14. op. cit. Crookenden, Napier. P.97.
15. Bando, Mark A. *The 101st Airborne in Normandy*. (Motorbooks International, Osceola, USA, 1994) p.30.
16. op. cit. Crookenden, Napier. p.108.
17. compiled from reports in *Utah Beach to Cherbourg Report, Drop Zone* by Brigadier-General S.L.A. Marshall and *Dropzone Normandy* by Napier Crookenden.
18. Katcher, Philip. *US 101st Airborne Division, 1942-45*. (Osprey, London, 1978) p.10.
19. op. cit *Utah Beach to Cherbourg Report*. p.75.

CHAPTER SIX

TOUR OF BATTLEFIELDS, MEMORIALS AND CEMETERIES

Distance: approximately forty-five miles

St Mère Église

The most convenient place to start a tour in the area of operations for the American airborne and seaborne forces on the Cotentin Peninsular is at St Mère Église (refer also to Chapter 4). Not only does this quaint ancient market town offer a good selection of memorials and information for the battlefield tourist to find, all within easy walking distance, but there is also the excellent airborne museum, *Musée des Troupes Aéroportées*. In addition, St Mère Église also offers a good point from which to locate suitable accommodation, stock up on refreshments, buy souvenirs, books and memorabilia, and also visit the local *Tourisme Information Office*.

To begin this tour, park your vehicle in the car park beside the church in the town square. This can be found by following the signs for St Mère Église while travelling on the **N13**.

If you are approaching St Mère Église from the south-east (from the direction of Bayeux), cross over the **D67** junction and on your right you will see Le Sainte-Mère Hotel. This is a reasonably priced two-star hotel which offers accommodation and meals. Adjacent to the hotel, on the left hand side of the road, there is the (**1a**) 505th PIR & General J.M. Gavin Sign and the (**1b**) 505th Parachute Regimental Combat Team Memorial, which was dedicated by the 505th RCT Association to honour those who liberated St Mère Église at 04.30 hrs on the 6 June 1944. Continue along the Rue Géneral de Gaulle to the south-west side of the town square passing, on your right, the military memorabilia and material store called *Static Line*. This store offers a selection of books, military uniforms, badges and artifacts, both original and reproduction, for sale; in addition there is also reproduction equipment, used in the Steven Spielberg film *Saving Private Ryan*, on display and for sale.

(**1a**) See Appendix D for list of monuments and memorials

If you approach St Mère Église from the north-west (from the direction of Cherbourg) follow the signposts for St Mère Église, just before you enter the town, on your right, there are the (**1c**) 101st Airborne Division & General M.D. Taylor Sign and the (**1d**) 82nd Airborne Division & General M.B. Ridgway sign. Continue along the Rue Cap de Laine into St Mère Église and on the left is the (**1e**) *Hotel de Ville*, which is the local Mairie (Town Hall) and the first to be liberated by American troops on D-Day.

Quinéville

Montebourg

Fontenay-sur-Mer

D69

St Marcouf

Ravenoville
Marmion

D269

Azeville

D14 Fourcarville

N13

St-Germain-de-
Varreville

D115

D423

les Mézières

St-Martin-de-Varreville

D17

La Londe

D421

nfreville

St-Mére Église

D14

Turqueville

D913

Cauquigny

D15

La Fiére

D67

N13

D524

Chef-du-Pont

D115

River Merderet

Les
Forges

St-Marie-du-Mont

D70

D329

Hiesville

D329

D913

D129

D913

Beúzeville-la-Bastille

D424

le
Gran
Vey

Vierville

Houtteville

St-Côme-du-Mont

River Douve

Brévands

River Séves

Carentan

UTAH BEACH

**Tour of Battlefields,
Memorials
& Cemeteries**

Inside there is the Stars and Stripes flag that was raised by Lt-Col Edward Krause when the town was liberated and various certificates and plaques dedicated to the American forces that liberated St Mère Église. Outside, in front of the Mairie, is the (**1f**) Civilian 1939-1945 War Memorial which commemorates the forty-five civilians who died during the fighting. The memorial also proclaims that St Mère Église was the first town to be liberated in France during the night of the 5/6 June, 1944 (a claim that is equally made by the people of Ranville and the men of the British 13th Parachute Battalion, 6th Airborne Division, who landed on the eastern flank of the invasion force).

In front of the civilian memorial is (**1g**) Km 0 the first of many marker stones that form part of the Voie de la Liberté (Road to Liberty). The markers are spaced out at every kilometre through Normandy and have two starting points, the first at St Mère Église (Km 0) and the second at Utah Beach Km 00. The marker at Utah Beach leads to St Mère Église, where the Road to Liberty continues in two directions; the first heading north to Cherbourg and the second south through Carentan and onto St Lô. The markers then continue south-west onto St Malo then south to Rennes, and east to Angers, Le Mans, Charters, Reims, Verdun and Metz. The route then heads north, through Luxembourg, and finishes in Bastogne in Belgium (for more details obtain Michelin, Road to Liberty, Map 105).

In the garden to the right of the Mairie there is the (**1h**) Generals Ridgeway and Gavin Memorial which was erected by the local people in honour of the two generals. From the Mairie continue along the Rue Cap de Laine, which then runs into the Rue Général de Gaulle on the south side of the town square.

From the Rue Général de Gaulle, take the Rue du Général D.D.

Some of the uniforms and equipment used in the film 'Saving Private Ryan' now on display and for sale in the store 'Static Line'.

Eisenhower, next to the *Tourisme Information* office, and park next to the church.

A visit to the *Tourist Information* office will provide you with further details about local museums. Also available is a detailed street map (plan de la ville) of St Mère Église. This map will provide you with additional details of local monuments and memorials. In addition, also ask for the information leaflet titled (**1i**) *St Mère Église Circuit Historique*. This leaflet will provide you with the location of fifteen information boards, erected in 2000 around St Mère Église, which display photographs of the area taken during the war and also information about the area in both English and French. Included in the *Circuit Historique* is a visit to the (**1j**) U.S. Cemetery Marker No 1 which can be found by taking the Rue du 505 Airborne, on the north-east of the town square and following the signpost for Collège Exupéry/Complexe Sportif.

This is the first of three US cemetery markers in the area that mark the location of the three temporary cemeteries that were established and tended between 1944 and 1948. At this location some 3000 Americans were buried before they were either repatriated to the United States or transferred to the Normandy American Military Cemetery at Colleville-sur-Mer (see Appendix C). The first burials were made on 10 June, 1944, when Major-General Lawton Collins designated the cemetery at St Mère Église as the VII Corps Cemetery. The cemeteries were operated by the 603rd Quartermaster Graves Registration Company who were initially helped by local civilians in digging the graves. However, more hands were soon needed as the number of dead quickly rose and German prisoners-of-war were also assigned to help in the burials.

General J. Lawton Collins visited the cemetery often, as did all the division commanders. During each visit General Collins

140

made it quite clear that all remains at the cemetery would be buried each day. This made for long and very hard days for Graves Registration personnel, guards and prisoners alike. This was especially true during the early days when we were in the 'on-the-job training' mode. We learned quickly how to handle remains with reverence, whether loading 30 to 35 remains in a one ton trailer, up to 110 on a two-and-a-half ton truck, or burying 200 or more remains at the cemetery in a single day.

Sergeant Charles D. Butte, 603rd QM Graves Registration Company.

Additional places of interest in St Mère Église are (**1k**) St Mère Église Church which has inside two beautiful stained glass windows dedicated to the US airborne forces. Also inside the church is a framed transcript of *A Paratrooper's Prayer*, written by a former chaplain of the 82nd Airborne Division, The Reverend

Chaplain Captain Francis L. Sampson at one of the temporary burial grounds.

(Major) George B. Wood. The prayer has also been translated into French and German.

Opposite the church entrance, across the car park and road, Rue Robert Murphy, can be found another military souvenir store the *Au Jour J.* A third military store is located on the south-west corner of the town square and is called *US Surplus.* Also to the south-west side of the town square, along the Rue Général de Gaulle (**1l**) Comité du Débarquement Memorial, one of the ten monuments raised by the French organisation that is dedicated to preserving the memory of the Normandy invasion.

About twenty yards to the right of the monument is the (**1m**) Alexandre Renaud Memorial. This is dedicated to the historian and former mayor of St Mère Église Alexandre Renaud who died in 1966 age 75 years. Monsieur Renaud was the mayor of St Mère Église on 6 June, 1944.

Opposite the church on the east side of the town square is the (**1n**) *Musée de Troupes Aéroportées* (see Appendices D & E) in which can be found many more memorials dedicated to the airborne troops.

Finally the (**1o**) 'C' Company, 505th PIR Memorial Plaque can be found by taking the Rue Général de Gaulle, on the south corner of the town square, and heading south-east toward the N13. Go past the *Static Line* store on your left, and take the first right down the Rue de la Cayenne. Three-quarters of the way along the road, on the left, is a house with the memorial plaque which is dedicated to the memory of four troopers; Sergeant William S. Smith, Private First Class William Walter, Private Robert L. Herrin and Private Robert E. Holtzmann, who were killed in action in St Mère Église on the 6 June 1944.

la Fière, Cauquigny & Chef-du-Pont

From St Mère Église drive back down Rue du Général D.D. Eisenhower, turn right onto the Rue Général de Gaulle and take the second left onto the Rue de Verdun. After passing under the road-bridge (N13) there is a fork in the road, where the right fork (D15) goes to la Fière and Cauquigny

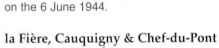

(see Chapter 4). Take the left fork (D67) and after approximately 120 Yards, on the left, is (**2d**) US Cemetery Marker No 2 which was the temporary burial ground of some 5,000 American soldiers. Amongst them was Brigadier-General Theodore Roosevelt Jr., the eldest son of the of the 26th President of the United States, and also cousin to the then serving President Franklin Delano Roosevelt.

Brig-Gen Roosevelt had died as a result of a heart-attack only seven days after the D-Day invasion, on the 12 June, 1944. He had been denied the opportunity of accompanying his men onto, the beaches after a verbal request to his commanding officer, Major-General Raymond O. Barton, was refused. However, his written request was finally accepted and, despite his failing health, Brig-Gen Roosevelt led the first waves of troops from the US 4th Infantry Division onto Utah Beach, becoming not only the first general to land on the Normandy beaches on D-Day but also the oldest at the age of fifty-six. Brig-Gen Roosevelt is now buried at the Normandy American Cemetery at Colleville-sur-Mer (see Appendix C). Another American soldier who was also buried at this site was Sergeant Joseph Z. Pritchett, 531st ESB. However, his body was later repatriated to the United States, upon the request of the family (and at the US Government's expense), along with over 9,300 other American servicemen who had been killed and temporarily buried near St Mère Église.

508th PIR, 82nd A/B Div. memorial garden at Chef-du-Pont.

Continue along the **D67** to Chef-du-Pont, when you enter the village, on the right is **Rue de l'Église** which leads to the village church. In the churchyard, at the base of the First World War Monument is (**2e**) 508th PIR and Rex Combs Plaque.

Return to the **D67** and continue onto the **D70** stopping before the bridge over the River Merderet. On your left is the (**2f**) 508th PIR Memorial Garden. Beside the pathway through the garden there is a memorial to the 508th PIR, 82nd Airborne Division, and a Normandie Terre-Liberté information board which describes the Americans' progress through Chef-du-Pont and towards Pont l'Abbé. Opposite the memorial garden, on the north side of the road, there is another monument which is the (**2g**) 508th PIR Memorial.

Like the crossing at la Fière the Germans put up strong

resistance against the Americans and the bridge was not secured until the 10 June, 1944. The fighting then continued, with reinforcements from the 358th Infantry Regiment, 90th Infantry Division, who advanced over the River Merderet towards their objective at Pont l'Abbe. This village was liberated two days later but only after a heavy Allied bombing raid had finally softened up the German defences.

les Forges, Turqueville & les Mézières

From the memorial garden head back towards **Chef-du-Pont** and take the **D70** on the right, towards St Marie-du-Mont. Just before the flyover, which crosses the **N13**, on the right is (**3a**) US Cemetery Marker No 3. This cemetery marker, at les Forges, marks the site where some 6,000 American Servicemen were temporarily buried. This site was selected by another member of the 603rd QM Graves Registration Company whose glider had crash landed nearby.

After studying the surrounding terrain, I went to one corner of the field and stuck my heel in the ground. This would be the upper left corner of the first grave. I found an empty K ration carton and split it into wooden stakes. I paced off the graves in rows of twenty and marked them with stakes. I had no transport, tape measure, shovels, picks or any other equipment... I also lacked burial bags (mattress covers), grave registration forms or personal effects bags. The situation rapidly exceeded what had originally been planned for the one-man graves registration unit and this was still the first day.

Sergeant Elbert E. Legg, 603rd QM Graves Registration Company.

Continue along the **D70**, over the **N13**, and take the second turning on the left, along the **D129** to **Turqueville**. Stop at the crossroads where there is a signpost showing that Turqueville is 0.3 km straight ahead. To your front and left is a chateau, this is the site where Private Wilbur Shanklin, 506th PIR, 82nd Airborne Division had his picture taken just after D-Day. The photograph was published in the *Sunday Graphic* on 11 June, 1944, and accompanied by an article by the British war correspondent Leonard Mosley. As a matter of fact, Mosley's article was actually referring to the British paratroopers as he had dropped with the British 9th Parachute Battalion, 6th Airborne Division, north-east of Caen. Nevertheless, these types of stories and pictures were regularly used as means of Allied propaganda.

Drive straight across the crossroads, along the **D129**, through Turqueville and Reuville. At the next crossroads take the **D423** to

506th PIR, 101st A/B Div. trooper, Wilbur W. Shanklin with a German prisoner.

Irena Zientek stands in for the German prisoner at Turqueville.

les Mézières. The farm buildings on either side of the road at les Mézières are those which were used by the Germans as a barracks, codenamed 'WXYZ,' and which were attacked by Staff-Sergeant Summers.

At the next crossroads take a right turn, onto the **D14**, find a safe place to park and walk back towards the crossroads. On your left there is a white road marker bearing the name of Pfc M. Prokopovich, 531st ESR. Farther along, to your right, on the north corner of the crossroads are two similar road markers that also bear the names of two other US Engineers. These are just three of some eighty-three road markers, in this area, that are dedicated to the forty-three US Engineers from the

VII Corps command post.

1st ESB, who were killed in the Normandy Campaign (see Appendix F for a full list and locations). As you continue the tour you will see many more such markers by the side of the road.

Continue to drive for approximately 250 yards past the next crossroads and look for a gateway and drive on your left which has, on the entrance posts, two (**3b**) VII Corps Command Post Plaques. These plaques, one in English and one in French, proclaim that the house at the end of the driveway was established by Major-General Joseph Lawton Collins, VII Corps Commander, as the first Command Post of the American Army in France.

Hiesville & St Marie-du-Mont

Continue along the **D14** for another 750 yards and turn right onto the **D524**. Drive to the end of the road and turn right onto **D70** and take the first left onto the **D129**. Take the second left onto the **D329**, signposted Hiesville, and just round the corner, on the left, is the (**4a**) Brigadier-General Don F. Pratt Memorial. The field behind the memorial is where Brig-Gen Pratt's glider, *The Flying Falcon*, crash landed and Pratt, the 101st Airborne Division's Assistant Commander, was killed.

Continue up the narrow road, **D329**, to Hiesville and find a suitable place to park near where the **D329** bends sharply to the right. Just after the corner, on the left, is the entrance to a house

Field where the 'Flying Falcon' crash landed.

Brig-Gen. Pratt memorial Hiesville.

Major-General Taylor's HQ. at Hiesville.

Major-General Maxwell D. Taylor at his command post at Hiesville June 1944.

which has on the right-hand gatepost the (**4b**) 101st Airborne Division Command Post Plaque. This plaque states that Major-General Maxwell D. Taylor established the first Command Post of the American airborne troops in this house.

To the left of the house is a narrow lane that leads down to the grounds of le Château Colombière. This is the site where the 101st Airborne Division set up its hospital on D-Day. However, the Chateau came under near constant artillery and sniper fire for several days after the landings and on the 9 June, 1944, the Luftwaffe, on one of its rare appearances dropped two bombs on the site. Though there were a number of casualties, many of the wounded in the area had fortunately been sent down to Utah Beach for evacuation. The chateau was so badly damaged during the fighting that it was demolished and replaced with a modern building after the war. The courtyard opposite the site of the chateau, which is made up of three large farm buildings, was also used later as a prisoner-of-war compound by the 101st Airborne Division.

From Hiesville continue past the former 101st Airborne Division Command Post on the **D329**, turn left at the T-junction onto the **D 329 E** and continue until you reach the crossroads with the **D70**. Turn right and then park near the church in St Marie-du-Mont. Almost opposite the church entrance, on the south-west side of the village square, is *la Boutique du Holdy* which is a store specializing in military memorabilia and

Major-General Maxwell D. Taylor, receiving the DSO from General Montgomery.

The grounds of le Château Colombière and a comparison

souvenirs. Also available from the store, for a small fee, is booklet called (**4c**) *La Nuit des Paras* à Sainte-Marie-du-Mont (Night of the Paratroopers at St Marie-du-Mont), which contains a map, and English translation, of fifteen plaques that are located at various points around the village. These plaques explain the battle that took place in St Marie-du-Mont during the night of the 5/6 June, 1944.

On the west side of the village Square there is also the local Tourist Information Office, and a *Normandie Terre-Liberté* information board which also has details of what happened in St Marie-du-Mont. On the north side of the square is the Hôtel Restaurant *L'Estaminet*, a small but pleasant hotel which offers reasonably priced accommodation and meals.

From St Marie-du-Mont take the southern road, the **D913** signposted Vierville, and drive out of the village. Take the next turning left, onto the **D424**, and after approximately 800 yards on the left is the (**4d**) US 36th Fighter Group Memorial. This memorial marks the site of the 9th USAAF Advance Landing Ground which

101st A/B Div. in St Marie-du-Mont and a comparison shot today.

Casualties around St Marie-du-Mont.

was built by the 843rd Air Engineer Battalion, and was in operation from the 5th to the 27 August, 1944.

Utah Beach

Continue along the **D424** and take the next left, onto the **D329**, and drive through **Brucheville** until you reach a T-junction with the **D115**. Turn left and then take the second turning on the right, onto the **D913**, and follow the road (**Exit 2**) down towards Utah Beach. Some 700 yards after the dogleg in the road there is, on the right side, the (**5a**) Danish Memorial which commemorates the 800 Danes who were involved in the D-Day landings.

Follow the **D913** down towards Utah Beach and take the next left

Men of the 1st ESB leaving the Chapelle de la Madeleine and how it looks today.

Utah Beach Museum.

which is signposted la Madeleine. 600 yards on your right is a small church which is the (**5b**) **Chapelle de la Madeleine**. This chapel was used by the troops during the Normandy campaign and inside there are dedications to the Allied troops including a stained-glass window.

Return to the **D913**, turn left and then turn right, at the end of the road and park in the large car park which is opposite the (**5c**) Utah Beach Musée (see Appendix D & E). To the right of the museum there is a Landing Craft Vehicle Personnel (LCVP) and two Alligator tracked vehicles. To the left of the museum there is a Sherman tank, a 90mm anti-aircraft gun and, on top of the sand-dune, examples of one type of beach defence used by the Germans. Called hedgehogs, these spiked steel objects were used

Some of the exhibits inside the Utah Beach Museum.

What is left of the German beach defences today at Utah Beach.

all along the Normandy coastline in 1944 in an attempt to deter any Allied invasion.

In front of the Utah Beach Museum there is the (**5d**) US 4th Infantry Division Monument. To the left of the museum there is a tall, red granite obelisk which is the (**5e**) Utah Beach U.S. Federal Monument which commemorates the achievements of VII Corps. This area has been developed as a small park built on part of the bunker system that formed part of the German fortification known as W5. Opposite the federal monument is the (**5f**) US 90th Infantry Division Memorial which is dedicated to all the units of the 90th Infantry Division that served in five campaigns, for 315 days from 6 June, 1944 to 5 May, 1945.

The stone steps lead up to the (**5g**) 1st Engineer Special Brigade Memorial which has been erected in memory of those engineers who lost their lives in the Normandy landings. Just beyond the engineer monument is a German 50mm FLAK *Flugabwehrkanone* anti-aircraft gun. Around the edge of this area, on the wall there is a series of directional plaques that give the distance and direction of a number of warships that were used during the Utah Beach landings as well as information on other places of interest.

(5f) US 90th Inf. Div. memorial.

Beneath the memorial, inside the bunker, a crypt has been formed in which all the names of all the men who were killed, from the 1st ESB, have been inscribed on the walls. The engineer memorial design was initially proposed by Colonel Caffey and on the wall opposite the crypt entrance is a (**5h**) Major-General Eugene Mead Caffey Memorial Plaque. Major Caffey died on the 30 May 1961. Other plaques nearby include the (**5i**) Souvenir Français, (**5j**) 1st ESB Headquarters Plaque and the (**5k**) US Coast Guard Combat Veterans Plaque.

Back towards the museum, just in front of the gap in the sand dunes which leads down to Utah Beach, there is (**5l**) Km 00, which is the second starting point for the *Voie de la Liberté* (Road to Liberty). On the left hand side of the gap in the sand dunes is the (**5m**) D-Day 40th Anniversary Plaque which lists a number of dignitaries who attended the 40th anniversary celebrations in 1984. From the beach it is possible to see, off-shore and to the north, the Iles St Marcouf. Also visible, though only at low tide, are the

Wreckage still evident on Utah Beach today, in the distance is the Utah Beach Museum built on the former German fortification known as W5.

wrecked remains of some of the thirteen blockships, codenamed 'Gooseberry,' that had been scuttled during Utah Beach landings. These merchant ships were sunk in order to provide Utah Beach with an effective breakwater which would aid the landing of supplies, material and men onto the beach. Only two large ship wrecks can be seen today, however, a walk along the beach during the low spring tides can reveal some surprising bits of wreckage that have survived for over half a century. Incidently, the rows of wooden poles seen at low tide are not part of *Generalfeldmarschall* Rommel's anti-invasion defences, they are, instead, just stakes put in by local fishermen for sea mussels. Nevertheless, at low tide the broken-off remains of some of the wooden beach defences can still be found in some places along the beach.

Back off the beach, opposite the gap in the sand dunes, is a short lane, called *Voie du Général Eisenhower*, which leads onto the **D913** and a restaurant called *Le Roosevelt*. This restaurant, bar and internet café, also has a souvenir shop, but, most interesting of all, it is built on a German bunker which, after its capture, was used by the navy as a communication centre. The owner of the restaurant, Monsieur Franck Méthivier, has done a wonderful job in preserving and recreating the bunker as it was back in 1944 and a free tour can be arranged by asking at the bar. Also inside the restaurant are a number of artifacts and military memorabilia which give the restaurant and bar an interesting and

The Bunker back in 1944.

Le Roosevelt Restaurant today.

relaxing atmosphere to have refreshment before continuing your tour of the battlefields.

On the 50th Anniversary of the landings, some returning veterans had a pleasant surprise when they were invited to look around the bunker which, in 1994, was being used as a wine cellar.

Our Navy shore group of NOIC (Naval Officer in Charge) set up radio communications operations in a German blochaus (we called it a bunker)... Our group, mostly radiomen, maintained communications there for about four months, from June 6/7 to at least the end of October, 1944. Ray Acosta and myself found our old bunker and with the permission of Evelyne Méthivier, the owner's sister, we, along with our wives, investigated to determine if the wine cellar was indeed our old bunker. Upon walking in we immediately knew that it was. But, more important, we started to find names of many of our buddies written randomly here and there on the walls. My wife, Vivian, found the last name... mine. We found about sixteen names from our group which numbered about 36 sailors who worked there regularly. I still find it hard to believe that the names have not faded away after more than 55 years.

Roger Chagnon and Charles Tumasz in front of their foxhole June, 1944.

Radioman 1st Class Roger L. Chagnon, Command Task Group 127-4, U.S. Navy.

Though much of their work was carried out in, and around, the relative safety of the bunker on the site of W5, the naval personnel had to spend the rest of their time living and sleeping in tent covered foxholes around Utah Beach; places that offered little protection from the German bombing raids and artillery bombardments that still continued in the area after D-Day.

Tent covered foxholes, Utah Beach 6th June, 1944.

German 50mm PAK (Panzerabwehrkanone) anti-tank gun in its concrete pit overlooking Utah Beach.

In the area to the right of the Utah Beach museum, beyond the landing craft, there is another German bunker, set into the sand dunes, that has now been converted into a public convenience. Above, on top of the sand dunes, there can be found the remains of a German 50mm PAK *Panzerabwehrkanone* anti-tank gun, in its concrete pit, overlooking Utah Beach. Farther south-east is the **(5n)** US Naval Reserve Memorial, dedicated to those who died on Utah Beach.

Return to the car park, the fields to the south-west of the car park are the area on which it is planned the Wall of Liberty (see Introduction) will be built. Drive past the museum, heading north, along the D421 up towards Hameau Mottet. On either side of the road, as you drive along, you will see evidence of the German fortifications. On the right there is a parking area and the **(5o)** Leclerc Monument. This area has one of the Comité du Débarquement monuments and, along the pathway four polished stone monuments dedicated to the 2nd French Armoured Division. Formed in Africa in 1941 the 2nd French Armoured Division, under the command of Général Leclerc, landed on Utah Beach 1 August, 1944. The Division soon formed part of Lieutenant-General George S. Patton's US Third Army and eventually liberated Paris on the 25 August, 1944. Also in this tended area of beach are examples of two armoured vehicles, a half-track and armoured car, used by the French Army during the liberation of France.

St Marcouf, Crisbecq & Azeville

Continue past the Leclerc monument and take the next left onto the **D423**, continue, through St-Martin-de-Varreville (nothing remains of the German battery that was sited at St Martin-de-Varreville), to the crossroads with the **D14** and turn right. Drive through St-Germain-de-Varreville and Foucarville and about 100 yards after leaving Foucarville, on the left, there is the **(6a)** German Prisoner-of-War Memorial Marker. This marks the site of a prisoner-of-war camp known as the 'Continental Central Enclosure

154

No 19' which was set up at the end of June, 1944. This massive complex housed some 40,000 German prisoners during the war and was like a small town with its own church, kitchens, warehouses, theatre, cinema, stadium and a 1,000 bed hospital. There were also 100 acres of arable land, used for farming, and a school where English, French, arithmetic, agriculture and manual skills were taught to help educate the German prisoners before they were released or transferred to other prisoner-of war camps. The camp was eventually decommissioned in 1947.

Continue along the **D14** to Ravenoville, on the right just before entering the village, opposite the **D15**, there is a small lane that leads down to Marmion. This is just one of the many farm buildings, used initially by the Germans, that were captured by the airborne troops and then used as a temporary base. Paratroopers, from both the 82nd and 101st Airborne Division, landed near this area in the early hours of D-Day and managed to capture Ravenoville from the local German garrison. During the initial fighting ten Germans were killed and thirty were taken prisoner and though the American casualties in this isolated battle are unrecorded the paratroopers managed to capture some German vehicles and a small ammunition dump.

Drive through Ravenoville, to St Marcouf, and take the narrow right hand lane down by the church and towards Crisbecq. At the end of the lane, at Crisbecq, turn left onto the **D69** and drive up the hill. On the left is an opening in the hedgerow which leads to a small car park.

This is the site of the Crisbecq Battery. Also known as the St Marcouf Battery, this site was to house four 210mm guns, one

Casemate at St Marcouf with its 210mm Skoda artillery piece prior to the Normandy invasion.

Paratroopers by St Marcouf church...

...and the same place today.

150mm gun and six 75mm anti-aircraft guns when finished. Though it was never fully completed, the site nevertheless did have three of its 210mm guns operational and a German garrison of some 400 men. This naval battery, commanded by *Oberleutnant* Ohmsen, had received a pounding from Allied bombers during the night of the 5/6th June with nearly 600 tons of bombs being dropped on and around the position of the battery.

However, despite this bombardment the Germans were still able to direct and fire their guns at the Allied invasion fleet and onto Utah beach during the invasion, managing to hit and sink the destroyer USS *Corry* (though it is also claimed that the destroyer hit a mine after it was hit by artillery fire which caused the ship to sink) and damaged many other vessels.

The German garrison managed to repel many Allied attacks on the battery, after the landings, until *Oberleutnant* Ohmsen finally gave the order to abandon the battery and withdraw, with just under eighty survivors, towards Cherbourg. The battery was finally taken on the 12 June

Paratrooper at St Marcouf church and the same place today on the lane that leads to the Crisbecq battery.

Paratroopers from the 82nd and 101st A/B Division use the farm building at Marmion, Ravenoville and the same place today.

by 2nd Battalion, 39th Infantry Regiment, 9th Infantry Division.

The remnants of the bunkers that housed the 210mm guns, can be seen in the fields across from the car park over the **D69**. These massive structures, known as casemate type H 683, allowed the 210mm guns to have a 120 degree field of fire and an elevation of 45 degrees. Though the guns have long since been removed the size and positions of the casemates provide the visitor with an impressive view of the Utah Beach area and the commanding position the Germans occupied for nearly a full week after the D-Day landings. This view is reinforced by climbing on top of the observation bunker, next to the car park, where on a clear day the village of Hameau du Sud, only one and a half miles away on the coast, and the Iles St Marcouf can be seen easily.

Continue west, on the **D69**, to the crossroads with the **D14**. Along the **D14** to the right, some 800 yards farther on and on the left hand side of the road, is the (**6b**) Advanced Landing Ground **A7** Memorial. This marks the site of an airfield built by the 365th Fighter Group, 9th USAAF, which was constructed and in operation between the 28 June and 15 August, 1944. Back at the crossroads continue west on the **D69** and then take the next left onto the **D269**. At the next T-junction turn right (still the **D269**) towards **Azeville**. On the left is the car park for the Batterie d'Azeville (see Appendix D). This battery had four 105mm guns and, because the coast could not be seen from this position, it was linked to the battery at Crisbecq.

The German garrison at Azeville numbered some 170 men

who managed to stop the Americans from taking the battery for three days despite heavy naval and aerial bombardments. On the 9 June a heavy artillery bombardment of some 1,500 shells, fired by the 44th Field Artillery Battalion, was laid down on the battery. This was immediately followed by an attack from the 3rd Battalion of the 22nd Infantry Regiment, 4th Infantry Division. During previous attacks though the Americans had themselves been shelled by the Battery at Crisbecq which had turned some of its guns on the perimeter of the Azeville Battery, nevertheless the Americans persisted with their attack and with the help of a tank, bazookas, pole charges and flame throwers, the German garrison was eventually overpowered and forced to surrender. The concrete bunkers at this battery which housed the 105mm guns are of two types. The larger two bunkers, located in the main area of the battery on the other side of the road from the car park, being a casemate type H 650 which also had a 38mm Flak gun mounted on top of the bunker.

Type H 650 Casemate at Azeville battery that housed 105mm guns.

Evidence of the damage done by Allied bombers and artillery.

From the battery drive through Azeville on the **D269** and continue to the T-junction with **D115**. Turn left and take the fourth turning on the right onto the **D17**. Some 700 yards past the entrance to la Londe Farm, on the right, there is the (**6c**) 552nd AAA/AW Battalion Memorial. This memorial is dedicated to the 552nd AAA/AW Bn. that protected the airfield which was built in the area of la Londe and became the first US Army Air Corp airfield in France. The airfield was built and in operation between the 12 June and 25 July 1944.

Finally, to complete your tour of the battlefields fought on by the American airborne and seaborne forces on D-Day, continue along the **D17** which will take you back into the town square of **St Mère Église**.

Additional Places of Interest

Orglandes German Cemetery

This German Cemetery is approximately seven miles from St Mère Église, and is located by taking the **D15**, due west, to Cauquigny. Then take the **D126**, through Amfreville to Orglandes and turn right onto the **D24**. The cemetery is some 600 yards on the left (see Appendix C).

la Cambe German Cemetery

This German cemetery is approximately nineteen miles from St Mère Église and is located by taking the **N13**, due south-east, towards Carentan and Bayeux. The cemetery is found on the southside of the **N13** some four miles after Isigny-sur-Mer (see Appendix C).

Normandy American Cemetery and Memorial

This American cemetery and memorial is approximately thirty-one miles from St Mère Église and is located by taking the **N13**, due south-east, towards Carentan and Bayeux. Some five miles after the German Cemetery at la Cambe, follow the signs for Formigny and then take the **D517** to St Laurent. Turn right onto the **D514** and the cemetery is located, just over a mile away, on your left (see Appendix C).

Quinville Musée de la Liberté

This Museum is approximately eleven miles from St Mère Église and is located by taking the **N13**, due north-west, to Montebourg, then the **D42**, east, to Quinville. Alternatively, a visit to this museum can be added onto the aforementioned tour after visiting the (6b) Advance Landing Ground Memorial near St Marcouf. From the memorial continue along the **D14**, through Fontenay-sur-Mer, until you reach the crossroads with the **D42** and turn right following the sign for Quinville (see Appendix E).

APPENDIX A

ALLIED ORDER OF BATTLE
6 June 1944

Commanders

Prime Minister, United Kingdom	Winston Churchill
President, United States of America	Franklin D. Roosevelt

Combined Chiefs of Staff

British Chiefs of Staff (COS)

Field Marshal Sir Alan Brooke
Admiral Sir Andrew B. Cunningham
Field Marshal Sir John Dill
Air Chief Marshal Sir Charles Portal
U.S. Joint Chiefs of Staff (JCS)
General Henry Arnold
Admiral Ernest J. King
Admiral William D. Leahy
General George C. Marshall

Supreme Headquarters,
Allied Expeditionary Force (SHAEF)

Supreme Commander	General Dwight D. Eisenhower
Deputy Supreme Commander	Air Chief Marshal Sir Arthur Tedder
Chief of Staff	Lt-Gen Walter Bedell Smith

Allied Strategic Air Forces

RAF Bomber Command	Air Marshal Arthur T. Harris
8th Air Force	Lt-Gen. James Harold Doolittle

Allied Expeditionary Air Force (AEAF)

Commander-in-Chief	Air Chief Marshal Sir T. Leigh-Mallory

Advance Force

RAF 2nd Tactical Air Force	Air Marshal Sir Arthur Coningham
US 9th Air Force	Lt-Gen Lewis H. Brereton
USAAF IX Troop Carrier Command (TCC)	Major-General Paul L. Williams
USAAF 50th Troop Carrier Wing	
USAAF 52nd Troop Carrier Wing	
USAAF 53rd Troop Carrier Wing	

Allied Naval Forces

Commander-in-Chief	Admiral Sir Bertram Ramsay
Western Naval Task Force	Rear-Admiral Alan G. Kirk
Task Force 'U'	Rear-Admiral Don P. Moon

Allied Ground Forces

Commander-in-Chief	General Sir Bernard Montgomery
US First Army	Lt. Gen. Omar Bradley
VII Corps	Major-General Joseph Lawton Collins

4th Infantry Division
Headquarters and Headquarters Company

Commander	Major-General Raymond O. Barton
Assistant Commander	Brig-Gen Theodore Roosevelt Jr. (died)
8th Infantry Regiment	Colonel James A. Van Fleet
12th Infantry Regiment	Colonel Russell P. Reeder

22nd Infantry Regiment   Colonel Hervey A. Tribolet
4th Engineer Combat Bn. (ECB)
4th Medical Battalion
4th Signal Company
4th Quartermaster Company
704th Ordnance Maintenance Company
4th Reconnaissance Troop
4th Military Police Platoon

HBB 4th Infantry Division Artillery
20th Field Artillery Battalion
29th Field Artillery Battalion
42nd Field Artillery Battalion
44th Field Artillery Battalion

82nd Airborne Division
Headquarters and Headquarters Company

Commander	Major-General Matthew B. Ridgeway
Assistant Commander	Brig-Gen James M. Gavin
505th Parachute Infantry Regiment	Colonel William E. Ekman
507th Parachute Infantry Regiment	Colonel George V. Millett
508th Parachute Infantry Regiment	Colonel Roy E. Lindquist
325th Glider Infantry Regiment	Colonel Harry L. Lewis
+ 2/401st GIR (aka 3/325th GIR)	
(seaborne)	Colonel Harry L. Lewis

307th Airborne Engineer Battalion
  (A & B Companies)
82nd Signal Company
307th Airborne Medical Company
407th Airborne Quartermaster Company
782 Airborne Ordnance Maintenance
  Company (OMC)
82nd Reconnaissance Platoon
82nd Military Police Platoon

HHB 82nd Airborne Division Artillery
80th AAA/AT Battalion
319th Glider Field Artillery Battalion
320th Glider Field Artillery Battalion
456th Parachute Field Artillery Battalion

90th Infantry Division	Brigadier Jay MacKelvie
359th Infantry Regiment (1 & 3rd Bn).	Clark K. Fales

101st Airborne Division
Headquarters and Headquarters Company

Commander	Major-General Maxwell D. Taylor
Assistant Commander	Brigadier-General Don Pratt (KIA)
501st Parachute Infantry Regiment	Colonel Howard R. Johnson
502nd Parachute Infantry Regiment	Colonel George V.H. Moseley Jr. (WIA)
	Lt-Col. John H. Michaelis
506th Parachute Infantry Regiment	Colonel Robert F. Sink
327th Glider Infantry Regiment (seaborne)	
+ 1/401 GIR (aka 3/327 GIR)	Colonel George S. Wear

326th Airborne Engineer Battalion
  (seaborne)
101st Airborne Signal Company

326th Airborne Medical Company
426th Airborne Quartermaster Company
801st Airborne Ordinance Maintenance
  Company (OMC)
101st Reconnaissance Platoon
101st Military Police Platoon

HHB 101st Airborne Division
81st Airborne AAA/AT Battalion
  (airborne and seaborne)
321st Glider Field Artillery Battalion
  (seaborne)
377th Parachute Field Artillery Battalion
  (seaborne)
907th Glider Field Artillery Battalion
  (seaborne)

6th Armoured Group	Colonel Francis F. Fainter
770th Tank Battalion	Lt-Col. John C. Welborn
746th Tank Battalion	Lt-Col C.G. Hupfer
749th Tank Battalion	
899th Tank Destroyer Battalion	
4th Cavalry Group	Colonel Joseph M. Tully
4th Cavalry Squadron	Lt-Col. E. C. Dunn
24th Cavalry Squadron	Lt-Col. F.H. Gaston Jr.
1st Engineer Special Brigade (ESB)	Brig-Gen James E. Wharton
Deputy Commander	Colonel Eugene M. Caffey
531st Shore Regiment	
1106th Engineer Group	
237th Engineer Combat Battalion	Major Herschel Linn
49th Engineer Combat Battalion	
299th Engineer Combat Battalion	
(B Company)	
238th Engineer Combat Battalion	

991st Engineer Treadway Bridge Company
612th Eng. Light Equipment Company
582nd Eng. Dump Truck Company
286th Joint Assault Signal Company
  (JASCO)

Naval Units attached to 1st ESB

Naval Combat Demolition Units (NCDU)	Lt. Commander Herbert Peterson
2nd Naval Beach Battalion	Lt. Commander John F. Curtin

Additional Supporting Units (seaborne)
65th Armored Field Artillery Bn. (AFA)
87th Chemical Mortar Battalion

49th Anti-Aircraft Artillery (AAA) Brigade
320th Barrage Balloon Battalion
  (VLA) (Coloured) Company C

11th AAA Group
116th AAA Gun Battalion
535th AAA Automatic Weapons (AW) Bn.
474th AAA AW Self Propelled (SP)

APPENDIX B

GERMAN ORDER OF BATTLE
6 June 1944

Commanders
Supreme Commander of the Armed
Forces & Commander-in-Chief of the Army   Adolf Hitler
Armed Forces High Command (OKW)
Chief   *Generaloberst* Wilhelm Keitel
Chief of Operations Staff   *Generaloberst* Alfred Jodl

Naval High Command
Commander-in-Chief   Grand Admiral Karl Dönitz
Naval Group West   Admiral Theodor Kranke

Air High Command
Commander-in-Chief   *Reichsmarschall* Hermann Goering
3rd Air Force   *Generalfeldmarschall* Hugo Sperrle

Commander-in-chief West (OB West)   *Generalfeldmarschall* Gerd von Rundstedt
Chief-of-Staff   *Generalleutnant* Guenther Blumentritt

Panzer Group West   General Leo von Geyr von Schweppenburg

Army Group B   *Generalfeldmarschall* Erwin Rommel
Chief-of-Staff   *Generalleutnant* Hans Speidel

7th Army   *Generaloberst* Friedrich Dollmann

84 Corps   General Erich Marcks

91st Luftlande Division   *Generalmajor* Wilhelm Falley
6th Parachute Regiment   Major Friedrich von der Heydte
1057 Grenadier Regiment
1058 Grenadier Regiment

243rd Infantry Division   *Generalleutnant* Heinz Hellmich
920th Grenadier Regiment
921st Grenadier Regiment
922nd Grenadier Regiment

352nd Infantry Division   *Generalleutnant* Dietrich Kraiss
914th Grenadier Regiment

709th Infantry Division   *Generalleutnant* Karl von Schlieben
Sturm Battalion A.O.K 7   Major Hugo Messerschmidt
649th Ost Battalion
   (attached to 729th Gren Regt)
729th Grenadier Regiment
739th Grenadier Regiment
795th Georgian Battalion
   (attached to 739th Gren Regt)
919th Grenadier Regiment
1261st Artillery Regiment

APPENDIX C

AMERICAN AND GERMAN CEMETERIES

CAMBRIDGE AMERICAN CEMETERY & MEMORIAL
Coton, Cambridge, CB3 7PH, England
Tel: 01954 210350   Fax: 01954 211130

In this thirty and a half acre cemetery, there are 3,811 headstones, arranged in a fan-shape of seven rows (A-G). There are 24 unknown service personnel buried, as well as two graves with two or three servicemen buried together (the latter marked by a bronze plaque). On a 472 foot long wall of Portland stone, to the south of the graves, there are inscribed the Tablets of the Missing, listing 5,126 service personnel missing in action. Amongst these names is Medal of Honor recipient, Leon R. Vance Jr., and also the name of USAAF Band leader Major Alton Glen Miller. The Memorial, at the west end of the Wall, features a mosaic ceiling, stained-glass windows and relief maps. This cemetery receives some 170,000 visitors each year.

The two men from the 505th PIR, 82nd Airborne Division, who were killed on the evening of the 5th June, 1944, are:

Pfc Robert L. Leakey interred in Plot E, Row 6, Grave 26.
Corporal Kenneth A. Vaught interred in Plot E, Row 5, Grave 26.
(see also Appendix F No 19).

NORMANDY AMERICAN CEMETERY & MEMORIAL
14710 Coleville-sur-Mer, France.
Tel: 02.31.51.62.00. Fax: 02.31.51.62.09.

Situated on the bluffs overlooking Omaha Beach and covering 172 and a half acres, this cemetery contains 9,387 graves including three Recipients of the Medal of Honor, 38 pairs of brothers, a father and son, and 307 unknowns. The Memorial is a semicircular structure with, in the centre, a statue, *The Spirit of American Youth Rising from the Waves*. Located behind this is the Garden to the Missing, which commemorates 1,557 service personnel missing in action. Near the centre of the cemetery there is a small circular chapel with a beautiful mosaic ceiling, and by the entrance to the cemetery there is a Visitors' Centre.
Over 1,250,000 people visit the cemetery each year.

Amongst the many servicemen interred in this cemetery are:
Colonel Ollie Reed in Plot E Row 20, Grave 19.
First Lieutenant Ollie Reed Jr. in Plot E, Row 20, Grave 20.
Brig-Gen Theodore Roosevelt Jr. in Plot D, Row 28, Grave 45.
Private Stanley Suwarsky in Plot F, Row 15, Grave 16.
Lieutenant-Colonel William L. Turner in Plot D, Row 19, Grave 21.
First Lieutenant Dennis T. Turner in Plot D, Row 19, Grave 22.
(also see Appendix E)

Normandy American cemetery memorial.

German cemetery at Orglandes.

ORGLANDES GERMAN CEMETERY

In this cemetery, inaugurated on 20th September 1961, there lie 10,155 German service personnel in 28 rows of graves. Each stone cross marks the final resting place of two or three servicemen. However, one of the graves bears 22 names, all killed on the same day by a dynamite explosion in Asnieres-en-Bassin
(Block 27, Row 13, Grave 420/1).

LA CAMBE GERMAN CEMETERY
14230 la Cambe, France.
Tel: 02.31.22.70.76

Originally the site of an American cemetery, and inaugurated a day after the Orglandes cemetery, there are over 21,115 German personnel interred here. The grass mound in the centre of the cemetery is a mass grave of over 250 men. Just before the entrance of the cemetery there is a pathway, opposite a Visitors' Centre, which runs through the Garden of Peace, as you walk amongst the trees there are polished stone markers inscribed with the numbers killed in all the major wars of the 20th century.

Graignes churchyard.

German cemetery at la Cambe.

APPENDIX D
MONUMENTS AND MEMORIAL PLAQUES

St Mère Église

(1a) 505th PIR & General J.M. Gavin sign.
(1b) 505th Parachute Regimental Combat Team Memorial
(1c) 101st A/B Division & General M.D. Taylor sign
(1d) 82nd A/B Division & General M.B.Ridgway sign
(1e) Hotel de Ville (Mairie)
 18th A/B Corps Plaque
 US Flag (first to be raised in France)
 Model of Liberty Ship, St Mère Église
 US Utah Industry Flag
(1f) Civilian 1939-45 War Memorial
(1g) Km 0
(1h) Generals Ridgway & Gavin Memorial
(1i) Circuit Historique
(1j) US Cemetery Marker No.1
(1k) Sainte-Mère Église Church
 505th PIR, 82nd A/B Div. 25th anniversary stained-glass window
 American paratrooper stained glass window
 Framed paratrooper's prayer
 Plaque dedicating church organ to the civilian and military victims of Second World War
(1l) Comité du Debarquement Monument
(1m) Alexandre Renaud Memorial
(1n) Musée de Troupes Aéroportées
 General Eisenhower Plaque
 Docteur Masselin Plaque
 Alexandre Renaud Plaque
(1o) C Company 505th PIR Memorial Plaque

La Fière, Cauquigny & Chef-du-Pont

(2a) Brigadier-General Gavin's foxhole
(2b) Bronze statue of 'Iron Mike'
(2c) A Company 505th PIR & 80th AAA/AT Bn., 82nd A/B Division bronze Plaques
(2d) US Cemetery Marker No. 2
(2e) 508th PIR & Rex Combs Plaque
(2f) 508th PIR Memorial Garden
(2g) 508th PIR Memorial

Les Forges, Turqueville & Les Mézières

(3a) US Cemetery Marker No. 3
(3b) 7th Corps Command Post Plaques

Hiesville & Sainte Marie-du-Mont

(4a) Brigadier-General Don F. Pratt memorial
(4b) 101st A/B Command Post Plaque
(4c) la Nuit de Paras à Sainte Marie-du-Mont Plaques
(4d) US 36th Fighter Group Memorial

Utah Beach

(5a) Danish Memorial
(5b) Chapelle de la Madeleine
 Jean Schwob d'Hericourt Plaque
 Free-French Force stained-glass window
(5c) Utah Musée
 Michel de Vallavieille Plaque
 238th Engineer Combat Bn. Plaque
 406th Fighter Group Plaque
 US Sea Service Personnel Commemorative Statue
(5d) US 4th Inf. Div. Monument
(5e) Utah Beach Federal Monument
(5f) US 90th Inf. Div. Memorial
(5g) 1st ESB Memorial
(5h) Major-General Eugene Mead Caffey Memorial Plaque
(5i) Souvenir Français
(5j) 1st ESB HQ Plaque
(5k) US Coast Guard Combat Veterans' Plaque
(5l) Km 00
(5m) D-Day 40th Anniversary Plaque
(5n) US Naval Reserve Memorial
(5o) Leclerc Monument

St Marcouf, Crisbeq & Azeville

(6a) German Prisoner of War Memorial
(6b) Advanced Landing Ground
(6c) 552nd AAA/AW Battalion Memorial

ADDITIONAL MEMORIALS

Barneville-Carteret

(a) 9th Inf. Div. Monument and Plaque (street intersection).

Carentan

(b) 502nd PIR, 101st A/B Div. Monument (west of Carentan on Highway 13).

(c) Comité du Debarquement Monument (in front of Mairie).

(d) 502nd PIR Plaque (base of Comité du Debarquement Monument).

(e) Inside Carentan Mairie: 101st A/B Division Flag and various 50th anniversary plaques and memorabilia.

(f) Carentan Church: 101st A/B Division stained-glass window.

(g) 11th Port HQ Plaque (4 Rue Sivard de Beaulieu).

COLOMBY
(h) 90th Infantry Division Memorial.

COUTANCES
(i) 4th Inf. Div. Plaque (town centre).

GRAIGNES
(j) 507th PIR, 82nd A/B Div. Bridge Plaque.

(k) Graignes Churchyard: 507th PIR Memorial Plaque, Franco-American Memorial Plaque, Memorial Plaque of civilian & military dead.

LA HAYE DU PUITS
(l) 749th Tank Battalion Plaque (on French War Memorial).

LE PLESSIS-LASTELLE
(m) C Company, 712th Tank Battalion Memorial.

(n) 90th Infantry Division Memorial.

LITHAIRE
(o) 82nd Airborne Division and 90th Infantry Division Memorial.

MAGNEVILLE
(p) 95th Squadron, 40th Troop Carrier Group, 9th USAAF, and 3/506th PIR 101st Airborne Division Memorial.

MÉAUTIS
(q) Brig-Gen. Roosevelt Jr. Plaque (in churchyard).

MONTEBURG
(r) 4th Infantry Division Plaque (on Rue de la 4e Division Infanterie Americaine, near Abbe).

ORGLANDES
(s) 9th & 90th Infantry Division 50th anniversary Plaque (on Orglandes Church wall).

PÉRIERS
(t) 359th Infantry Regiment, 90th Infantry Division Flag (in Mairie).

(u) 90th Infantry Division Plaque (on French War Memorial).

(v) 90th Infantry Division Monument.

PICAUVILLE
(w) 508th PIR Monument (on D 67).

SAINTENY
(x) 4th Infantry Division Monument.

SAINT-GERMAIN-SUR-SÈVES
(y) 90th Infantry Division Memorial.

(j) 507th PIR 82 A/B Div. bridge plaque, Graignes.

APPENDIX E – MUSEUMS

C-47 Dakota exhibit inside Airborne Museum, St Mère Eglise.

St Mère Église

Musée des Troupes Aéroportées (Airborne Troops Museum),
Place du 6 Juin, 50480 Sainte-Mere-Église.
Tel: 02.33.41.41.35. Fax: 02.33.41.78.87.

This museum, in the centre of the village, is dedicated to the men of the 82nd & 101st Airborne Divisions. It houses equipment and mementos of the airborne troops, including a C-47 Douglas Dakota and a

St Mère Église Airborne Museum.

Waco glider.
Open daily from February to November.

St Marie-du-Mont

Musée du Debarquement d'Utah Beach (The Utah Beach Landings Museum),
Utah Beach, 50480 Sainte-Marie-du-Mont.
Tel: 02.33.71.53.35. Fax: 02.33.71.93.30.

Set at the site of the landings on Utah Beach, this museum has displays of photos,

models and film archives, which tell the story of the American landings on Utah. Equipment, including a Sherman tank is exhibited outside the museum.
Open daily from April to November, and also at weekends between December and March.

Azeville

La Batterie d'Azeville (The Azeville Battery), 50310 Azeville.
Tel: 02.33.05.98.83. Fax: 02.33.05.98.16.

One of the earliest parts of the Atlantic Wall in la Manche, this battery once housed four 105 mm guns. It is sited near to the marine Battery of Crisbecq.
Open each afternoon between June and August.

The Museum of Freedom at Quineville.

Quineville

Musée de la Liberté (The Museum of Freedom),
Avenue de la Plage, 50310 Quineville.
Tel: 02.33.21.40.44. Fax: 02.33.21.52.20.

Depicting everyday life during the Occupation, through a reconstruction of an ordinary French street, rare photos and 52 minute film.
Open daily from March to November.

Cherbourg

Musée de la Libération (The Liberation Museum),
Fort du Roule, 50100 Cherbourg.
Tel: 02.33.20.14.12.

Located in the fort at the top of the Roule mountain, this museum covers the Occupation, the invasion and liberation of the Cotentin Peninsula.
Open daily during the season.

APPENDIX F
1st ENGINEER SPECIAL BRIGADE - ROAD MARKERS

1) Barone Road (2 markers). **Pvt F. Barone**, 519th Port Bn. KIA 10/06/44
   Location: D 421 Intersection with Chemin de la Madeleine, and Madeleine Chapel.
   Interred: Normandy American Cemetery, Plot B, Row 7, Grave 35.

2) Begel Road (2 markers). **T/4 W. Begel**, 519 Port Bn. KIA 15/06/44
   Location: D 243 & D 421, and Middle of D 423.
   Interred: Normandy American Cemetery, Plot H, Row 17, Grave 37.

3) Blair Road (2 markers). **Pvt J. Blair**, 4090th Qm Serv Co. KIA 10/06/44
   Location: D 67 & D 421, and D 67 Intersection with road to les Dunes.
   Interred: Normandy American Cemetery, Plot A, Row 1, Grave 37.

4) Bryant Road (2 markers). **Pfc D.S. Bryant**, 531st ESR. KIA 06/06/44
   Location: D 913 & Hartwell Road & Siezmore Road, and D 913 & D 14 & D 115.
   Interred: Repatriated USA.

5) Calandrella Road (2 markers). **Pvt G. Calandrella**, 531st ESR. KIA 06/06/44
   Location: D 421 & Beach Access Utah, and end of dune access – road off D 421 at Utah Beach.
   Interred: Normandy American Cemetery, Plot F, Row 9, Grave 31.

6) Carter Road (2 markers). **Pvt T.H. Carter**, 531st ESR. KIA 06/06/44
   Location: On D 219 from D 421 –½mile, and D 129 & D 14 Saint Germain-de-Ville.
   Interred: Repatriated USA.

7) Collins Road (2 markers). **Sgt W.L. Collins**, 490th Port Bn. KIA 06/06/44
   Location: D 14 just before intersection with D 524, and Intersection D 14 & D 913.
   Interred: Normandy American Cemetery, Plot F, Row 28, Grave 31.

8) Criss Road (2 markers). **T/5 J.H. Criss**, 531st ESR. KIA 06/06/44
   Location: D 423 & St-Martin-de-Varreville, and D 423 intersection with D 14.
   Interred: Normandy American Cemetery, Plot H, Row 10, Grave 37.

9) Curry Road (2 markers). **Pvt E.J. Curry**, 519th Port Bn. KIA 10/06/44
   Location: D 115 & D 329, and D 115 & le Grand Vey (end of road).
   Interred: Repatriated USA.

10) Danel Road (2 markers). **Pvt S. Danel**, 3207th Qm Serv Co. KIA 09/06/44
    Location: End of D 913, behind Le Roosevelt Restaurant Utah Beach & D 421, and D 913
    & la Madeleine Road – Stoute Road.
    Interred: Normandy American Cemetery, Plot C, Row 10, Grave 18.

11) Davis Road (2 markers). **T/4 W.O. Davis**, 815th Trk Co. KIA 10/06/44
    Location: ½ mile from D 421 on D 129, and Intersection of D 421 & D 219.
    Interred: Repatriated USA.

12) Effler Road (2 markers). **Pvt A.A. Effler**, 531st ESR. KIA 14/06/44
    Location: D 329 Pouppeville intersection with Miller Road, and D 329 intersection with
    McGowan Road.
    Interred: Repatriated USA.

13) Fitts Road (2 markers). **Pvt F.H. Fitts**, 519th Port Bn. KIA 15/06/44
    Location: D 115 & D 913 & D 14, and D 115 & D 329 – Pouppeville.
    Interred: Repatriated USA.

14) Ford Road (2 markers). **Pvt C. Ford**, 4090th Qm Serv Co. KIA 10/06/44
    Location: Between Saint Germain & Saint Martin, off D 14 intersection, 500 yards south
    of Gatt Road, and 500 yards from intersection with D 14.
    Interred: Repatriated USA.

15) Fottrell Road (2 markers). **1 Lt W.T. Fottrell**, 531st ESR. KIA 06/06/44
Location: D 421 les Hougues, and D 421 Leclerc Monument.
Interred: Normandy American Cemetery, Plot H, Row 1, Grave 37.

16) Gatt Road (2 markers) **Pvt W.E. Gatt Jr.**, 531st ESR. KIA 06/06/44
Location: D 14 $\frac{1}{4}$ mile south-east of Saint Germain-de-Varreville on intersection,
and 500 yards from intersection with D 14.
Interred: Repatriated USA

17) Glenn Road (2 markers). **Pvt W.L. Glenn**, 531st ESR. KIA 25/06/44
Location: on small road $\frac{1}{2}$ mile from intersection with D 421 & D 423, and D 421 & D 423.
Interred: Repatriated USA.

18) Goodman Road (2 markers). **Pvt R. Goodman**, 818th Trk Co. KIA 13/06/44
Location: D 14 & D 15, and D 14 & D 129.
Interred: Normandy American Cemetery, Plot F, Row 12, Grave 11.

19) Ham Road (1 marker). **Pvt O.A. Ham**, 531st ESR. KIA 10/06/44
Location: Middle 329.
Interred: Cambridge American Cemetery, Plot F, Row 0, Grave 37.

20) Hartwell Road (2 markers). **Pvt R.E. Hartwell**, 286th JA Sig Co. KIA 06/06/44
Location: D 913 & Pouppeville Road, and In Pouppeville.
Interred: Repatriated USA.

21) Hayes Road (2 markers). **Pvt J. O. Hayes**, 4090th Qm Serv Co. KIA 10/06/44
Location: D 67 intersection with D 14, and D 67 intersection with Long Road.
Interred: Repatriated USA.

22) Hetke Road (1 marker). **Sgt E.L. Hetke**, 531st ESR. KIA 10/06/44
Location: Off D 329 Beach road near Utah Beach Museum.
Interred: Normandy American Cemetery, Plot B, Row 8, Grave 30.

23) Hinkel Road (2 markers). **1 Lt R.A. Hinkel**, 816th Trk Co. KIA 14/06/44
Location: D 913 between Stoute Road and Danish Monument, with la Grande Dune, and
D 913 at Danish Monument.
Interred: Repatriated USA.

24) Holt Road (2 markers). **T/4 H.S. Holt**, 519th Port Bn. KIA 15/06/44
Location: Middle of D 17, and D 14 & D 17.
Interred: Repatriated USA.

25) Jones Road (2 markers). **Pfc C.O. Jones**, 261st Med Bn. KIA 06/06/44
Location: D 913 Km 10 Marker, and on D 913 at intersection with Pouppeville Road.
Interred: Normandy American Cemetery, Plot C, Row 21, Grave 40.

26) Leighton Road (2 markers). **Pvt F.K. Leighton**, 531st ESR. KIA 29/06/44
Location: Middle of D 17, and D 421 & D 17.
Interred: Normandy American Cemetery, Plot C, Row 25, Grave 27.

27) Long Road (2 markers). **Cpl J.A. Long**, 4090th Qm Serv Co. KIA 10/06/44
Location: On Chemin de Pierville & D 14 near Pierville, and on Chemin de Pierville near
(100 yards) intersection with D 67.
Interred: Normandy American Cemetery, Plot A, Row 18, Grave 37.

28) McGowan Road (2 markers). **Pfc W.F. McGowan**, 531st ESR. KIA 06/06/44
Location: 329 next to Ham Road, and 329 intersection with Effler Road.
Interred: Normandy American Cemetery, Plot A, Row 13, Grave 16.

29) Miller Road (2 markers). **Pvt W.A. Miller**, 261st Med Bn. KIA 07/06/44
Location: Pouppeville intersection with Houesville Road, and Houesville.
Interred: Repatriated USA.

30) Olle Road (2 markers). **T/5 S.J. Olle**, 531st ESR. KIA 06/06/44
   Location: Intersection with D 421 & D 913 at Monument, and D 421.
   Interred: Normandy American Cemetery, Plot F, Row 17, Grave 33.

31) Pritchett Road (2 markers). **Sgt J.Z. Pritchett**, 531st ESR. KIA 25/06/44
   Location: D 423 & Saint Martin-de-Varreville, and Middle of D 423.
   Interred: Repatriated USA

32) Prokopovich Road (2 markers). **Pfc M. Prokopovich**, 531st ESR. KIA 06/06/44
   Location: On D 14 & D 67, and on D 14 & D 423.
   Interred: Repatriated USA.

33) Pugach Road (2 markers). **1 Lt J.J. Pugach**, 286th Sig Co. KIA 11/06/44
   Location: On D 14 intersection with D 219, and on D 14 & D 423.
   Interred: Normandy American Cemetery, Plot D, Row 19, Grave 3.

34) Ridgeway Road (2 markers). **Pvt L.L. Ridgeway**, 519th Port Bn. KIA 10/06/44
   Location: D 421 & Beach access & la Madeleine, and D 421 & Beach access & la Madeleine Road.
   Interred: Normandy American Cemetery, Plot D, Row 12, Grave 25.

35) Robertson Road (1 marker). **Sgt L.M. Robertson Jr.**, 286th JA Sig Co. KIA 10/06/44
   Location: D 14 & D 15 Ravenoville.
   Interred: Repatriated USA.

36) Rowe Road (2 markers). **Pvt J.T. Rowe**, 531st ESR. KIA 06/06/44
   Location: Path to Beach between the Museum and Utah Beach Monument.
   Interred: Repatriated USA.

37) Siezmore Road (2 markers). **T/5 C.W. Siezmore**, 286th JA Sig Co. KIA 15/06/44
   Location: D 14 & road opposite D 524, and Intersection of D 913.
   Interred: Repatriated USA.

38) Simmons Road (2 markers). **Pvt J.H. Simmons**, 531st ESR. KIA 13/06/44
   Location: D 421 village Le Petit Hameau, and D 421 & D 15 Ravenoville.
   Interred: Normandy American Cemetery, Plot A, Row 16, Grave 26.

39) Slasinski Road (2 markers). **Pvt W.M. Slasinski**, 519th Port Bn. KIA 10/06/44
   Location: On D 67 & D 14, and D 67 1 mile from intersection with D 14.
   Interred: Repatriated USA.

40) Sonnier Road (2 markers). **Pfc L. Sonnier**, HQ Co, 1st ESB. KIA 06/06/44
   Location: D 913 & D 14, and D 913 in St-Marie-du-Mont.
   Interred: Repatriated USA.

41) Stoute Road (2 markers). **Pvt A.W. Stoute**, 4090th Qm Serv Co. KIA 10/06/44
   Location: Race track exit road, and D 913 & Stoute Road & la Madeleine Road at race track.
   Interred: Repatriated USA.

42) Walker Road (2 markers). **T/5 N.L. Walker**, 818th Trk Co. KIA 13/06/44
   Location: Route des Allies intersection with D 67 & D 421, and D 421 les Hougues.
   Interred: Repatriated USA.

43) Wall Road (2 markers). **1 Lt C.W.Wall**, 1st ESB. KIA 09/06/44
   Location: D 14 & D 524, and D 14 & D 67.
   Interred: Normandy American Cemetery, Plot F, Row 19, Grave 37.

APPENDIX G

CASUALTIES
CASUALTY FIGURES GIVEN IN VII CORPS G-1 REPORTS
6 JUNE 1944 - 1 JULY 1944

Division/unit	Killed	Wounded	Missing	Captured	Total
4th Inf Div	844	3,814	788	6	5,452
9th Inf Div	301	2,061	76	-	2,438
79th Inf Div	240	1,896	240	-	2,376
90th Inf Div	386	1,979	34	-	2,399
82 A/B Div	457	1,440	2,571	12	4,480
101st A/B Div	546	2,217	1,907	-	4,670
Corps Troops	37	157	49	61	304
Total	2,811	13,564	5,665	79	22,119